FIFTY SHADES OF HAY

FIFTY SHADES OF HAY

THE EXTRAORDINARY WORLD OF RACEHORSE NAMES

David Ashforth

RACING POST

First published in Great Britain in 2018 by Racing Post Books
27 Kingfisher Court, Hambridge Road, Newbury RG14 5SJ

10 9 8 7 6 5 4 3 2 1

ISBN 978-1-910497-71-5

Designed by J Schwartz & Co.

Printed and bound in the UK by Bishops

www.racingpost.com/shop

To all the horses who have risen above the silly names they have been given and to those owners who have given their horses jolly good names

CONTENTS

*The book will probably fall open at the above chapter. Surprisingly, it's not the longest.

ACKNOWLEDGEMENTS

Thank you to everyone who suggested names for inclusion, most of them rude.

I would like to say that any errors are entirely theirs but sadly they are entirely mine. Try not to take too much pleasure from pointing them out. Nobody likes a know-all.

So many people have helped that I might as well apologise now for missing you out. Sorry.

Particular thanks to the enthusiastic team at Racing Post Books – Brough Scott, Liz Ampairee, Julian Brown, James Norris and Stephen Griffin. Stephen suggested the title of the book, so that's his fault.

Thanks to Graham Coster for providing very capable and constructive editing without irritating the author and to Dan Barber and John Schwartz for their splendid design work. Also to Ian Greensill for his proofreading work.

The next thank you to those Twitterers who suggested names for inclusion, most of them legal.

Herewith, without discrimination between the very helpful and the hardly helpful at all and in reverse alphabetical order, in belated protest at teachers who picked on those with surnames beginning with 'A', thank you to: Barry Wright, Alison Wade, Dr Misha Voikhansky, Darren Thrussel, Jeff Thornbury, Joe Saumarez Smith, Jim Old, Denis Paul Murphy, Margo Miller, Martin Matthews, Sean Magee, Nicholas and Cherry Jones, Simon Holt, Richard Hoiles, Denis Hogan, Richard Henry, John Joseph Hanlon, Joanne Gunn, Lord Grimthorpe, Nick Godfrey, Jan Gardner, John Ferguson, Sheila Dixon, Steve Dennis, Dominic Ffrench Davis, Tim Cox, Mike Butts, Alan Burke, Sarah Barton, Michael Baldry, Bob Baffert and David Atkinson.

LIST OF ILLUSTRATIONS

PRE-START

Writing this has almost driven me mad. Perhaps it has. It's either driven me mad or almost mad. It's difficult to tell, with madness.

I have drowned in names. If you think they're the wrong names then please write a sequel, because there are plenty of names to go around. So try not to complain too much and since you've got the book you might as well read it, or give it away. Giving's good. Charity shops might take it.

ARE RACEHORSE OWNERS MAD?

You might feel sure that a horse is not a Flamingo, a Polar Bear, a Tomato, a Teapot, a pair of Bootlaces, a Taxidermist, a Rat Catcher or a Flea, but you'd be wrong. Racehorse owners often give their horses bizarre names that would seem to make success impossible.

Luckily, thoroughbreds are able to defy such handicaps. A Spaniel has won the Derby (1831), a Crow the St Leger (1976), a Butterfly the Oaks (1860) and, difficult to imagine, Oscar Wilde the Welsh National (1958). It's bonkers. Bonkers won at Southwell in 2002.

Over the centuries there have been hundreds of thousands of different names bestowed or inflicted on racehorses. You will wonder why some names have been included in this book and others left out. Well, that's the way it is.

ONLYFOOLSOWNHORSES (2011)
• Presenting • Lizzy Langtry (King's Theatre)

Did his best to prove himself wrong by winning three hurdle races in a row in 2017.

WHAT DOES THAT MEAN?

Racing's vocabulary is a bit like Chinese. If you are Chinese
it's pretty easy to understand. So here are some clues.

Pedigree   For instance, *Fiftyshadesofhay (2010) Pulpit –*
                         Quiet Kim (Real Quiet). Fiftyshadesofhay was
                         born in 2010. Pulpit is her father (sire), Quiet
                         Kim is her mother (dam) and Real Quiet is her
                         grandfather (grandsire) on her mother's side.

Flat race   A race with no obstacles to jump, making it less
                         likely that the horse you have backed will fall
                         over. It will have to think of some other way
                         to depress you.

Hurdle race   A race in which the horses are required
                         to jump hurdles.

Chase   A race in which horses are required to jump
                         fences, which are bigger than hurdles.

Selling race   A race in which the winner is offered for sale
                         at auction afterwards. The current owner may
                         no longer want the horse and neither, probably,
                         does anyone else.

Claiming race   A race after which any of the runners
                         can be bought for specified sums.

Handicap race   In Britain, most races are handicaps. Horses of differing abilities race against each other, carrying different weights based on their past performances. Theoretically, this gives them an equal chance of winning. The official handicapper's notion of heaven is a multiple dead heat, an outcome that is a punter's notion of hell.

Maiden race   A race for horses that have not yet won one and probably never will.

Bumper race   A Flat race for jumps horses.

Point-to-points   Race meetings staged by the hunting fraternity between December and June. The races are all chases, mainly over three miles, and the horses are ridden by amateur riders. Many of the horses have previously raced in 'normal' jumps races.

Hunter chases   Races for horses that have been hunting and probably running in point-to-point races, ridden by amateur riders and staged at 'normal' racecourses. The contestants are usually the better point-to-point horses.

Group races   Group 1, 2 and 3 races on the Flat and Grade 1, 2 and 3 races over jumps are at the top of racing's pyramid. In 2017 there were 36 Group 1 races in Britain, including the Derby, with Ascot and Newmarket staging 22 of them. During the 2017/18 jumps season, there were 40 Grade 1 races, including the Cheltenham Gold Cup, 25 of them at either Cheltenham or Aintree.

Immediately below them in the pecking order are Listed races.

Jockey   Small person devoted to driving you mad.

Trainer   Athletic coach employed by owners to maximise their horses' performance level and explain that their horse ran much better than it appeared to, despite finishing last, again.

Owner   Someone who believes that hope will eventually triumph over experience.

1. CHAMPIONS

Part 1

To qualify for inclusion it is neither necessary nor sufficient to be an equine superstar. My champions are not merely champions in deed but also champions in name; champions with a story.

CHAMPION THE WONDER HORSE

Champion the Wonder Horse! Champion the Wonder Horse!
Like a streak of lightnin' flashin' cross the sky,
Like the swiftest arrow whizzin' from a bow,
Like a mighty cannonball he seems to fly.
You'll hear about him everywhere you go.
The time'll come when everyone will know
The name of Champion the Wonder Horse!

Champion the Wonder Horse, played by three different horses, starred in almost 200 films and television programmes between 1935 and 1956 but not as a racehorse. He had too many letters.

The British Horseracing Authority has rules laying out restrictions on the names available for thoroughbreds. They include a rule banning names containing more than 18 characters, including spaces. You could have Championthewonderh but it's not quite the same. So, sadly, you'll have to cross out Champion the Wonder Horse.

Now you've defaced the book. Don't write in books! It's a horrible habit.

The long and the short of it

Eighteencharacters (2002)
- Honour and Glory • Cantare (Summer Squall)

Won once, at Tampa Bay in 2006.

Eighteencharacters (2013)
- Tribal Rule • Midnite Mama (Affirmed)

Has won four times so far, in California and Arizona.

I (1930)
- Yuyito • Bibesca (Camacho)

Reputed to have raced in Argentina during the 1930s, I wasn't really I but I with a ¿ on one side and ? on the other side. So it's fake news.

Fake News (2015)
- Paco Boy • Day Creek (Daylami)

Trained by David Barron, Fake News won at Carlisle at 25-1 in 2017 and at Wolverhampton at 8-1 in 2018. Honestly.

With I disqualified, the next best thing is:

So (1969)
- Little Buskins • Dutch Dish (Gilles De Retz)

Perhaps the owner, Mr De Vere Hunt, wanted to economise on letters. If so, it worked pretty well, because So won ten hurdle races and chases between 1974 and 1979 when trained by Edward O'Grady in Ireland. With old age approaching, he moved to England, which didn't seem to suit him, although So did complete the course in the 1981 Grand National, having failed to do so in the 1978 edition.

So had another claim to fame, as the first horse to be celebrated in verse by E J Thribb, *Private Eye* magazine's resident poet. *The Times* had reported, mistakenly, that So would miss the 1978 Grand National (see Fake News, above), prompting the following from Thribb:

So
Farewell then
So.
So.
A strange name
For a horse.
I wonder
If there is
A horse
Called 'Farewell'
– Or even 'Then'.
Imagine.
What a
Result.
1. So
2. Farewell
3. Then

Although So completed the course in 1981, his rider, seven times champion jump jockey John Francome, was not a fan. 'Not only was So small,' Francome recalled, 'he was a bad mover as well. He went down to the start like his legs were tied together. I should have been given a knighthood for getting that horse round.' As yet, Francome hasn't been.

ARKLE (1957)
• Archive • Bright Cherry (Knight Of The Garter)

Everyone's heard of Arkle. Well, everyone past retirement age.

The greatest chaser that ever lived was named after a mountain on his owner Anne, Duchess of Westminster's Scottish estate. As the mountain is a modest 787 metres high, it might have been more appropriate to have called him Everest, a more fitting 8,848 metres high. On the other hand, the Duchess didn't own Everest and pilgrims stand a better chance of reaching the top of Arkle, now owned by the Duke of Westminster. He owns most things but not racehorses. It might be worth asking him to marry you: then you can ask him to buy some.

Uniquely, Arkle could be reached by sending a letter addressed simply to 'Arkle, Ireland', where he was known as 'Himself'.

It's only ArkleArkleArkleArkleArkle – Arkle, that's all –
Arkle the whole way.
Twinny Byrne on being asked about conversation in an
Irish pub.

Races won: Cheltenham Gold Cup 1964, 1965, 1966; Irish Grand National 1964; Hennessy Gold Cup 1964, 1965; Whitbread Gold Cup 1965; King George VI Chase 1965, plus 19 other races. Amazing.

A jolly good name

Wait For The Will (1996)
• Seeking The Gold • You'd Be Surprised (Blushing Groom)
Bred by Paul Mellon when in his 90s. A wealthy Anglophile American, Mellon was the owner-breeder of many top class horses, including Mill Reef, winner of the 1971 Derby; Sea Hero, winner of the 1993 Kentucky Derby; and champions Arts And Letters and Fort Marcy. An unassuming man, Mellon was evidently exasperated by speculation about his posthumous dispensations before he was posthumous.

The day my final race is run
And, win or lose, the sinking sun
Tells me it's time to quit the track
And gracefully hang up my tack,
I'll thank the Lord the life I've led
Was always near the thoroughbred.
Paul Mellon, 1975

Races won: Wait For The Will ran only twice for Mellon before the owner's death in 1999. He subsequently won 16 times for trainer Gary Moore.

Another jolly good name

Au Renoir (2010)
• Peintre Celebre • Goodbye (Efisio)
Deserved to do better with such a clever name but failed to win, albeit from only four attempts. Was much better at painting.

ARROGATE (2013)
• Unbridled's Song • Bubbler (Distorted Humor)

Named after a spa town in Yorkshire (I'm guessing), Arrogate headed the World Racehorse Rankings in 2016 and again in 2017. In both years he was also the biggest earner of prize money. Staggeringly (well, I'm staggered, anyway), in his 11 career starts he won an average of $1.6 million (£1.2 million) per race and a total of over $17.4 million (£13.2 million). Not that Prince Khalid Abdullah, the owner of Arrogate's owner, Juddmonte Farms, needed the money, although every little helps.

Seven million dollars (£5.3 million) came from winning the first running of the world's most valuable race, the Pegasus World Cup Invitational Stakes. Staggeringly (see above) to European eyes, runners not using Lasix (furosemide), a drug used to prevent bleeding, banned in Europe, were given a 5lb weight allowance, an incentive that persuaded the connections of only one of the 12 runners to dispense with the drug. In 2018 the allowance was raised to 7lb and none of the dozen runners abandoned Lasix. They could try 9lb.

It makes you think but then so does the fact that the sun will burn up in a few billion years' time and then where will we be?

That's the greatest horse I've ever seen run. I can't believe
he won. When they turned for home I told myself, 'If he
wins, this is the best horse we've seen since Secretariat.'
*Trainer Bob Baffert after Arrogate won the 2017 Dubai World
Cup, starting slowly and coming from last to first.*

Races won: seven races including 2016 Grade 1 Travers Stakes and
Breeders' Cup Classic; 2017 Pegasus World Cup and Dubai World Cup.

BENNY THE DIP (1994)
* Silver Hawk * Rascal Rascal (Ack Ack)

The 1997 Derby winner, owned by the splendidly named
Charles Landon Knight II and trained by John Gosden, had
a cracking name.

Benny The Dip was widely believed to be a Damon Runyon
character but was he? It was claimed that he was named after
a character in the musical adapted from Runyon's book of stories,
Guys and Dolls, but that was Benny Southstreet.

Benny The Dip was said to have appeared in 'A Very Honorable
Guy', one of Runyon's earliest short stories, first published
in *Cosmopolitan* magazine in August 1929, but he isn't there.
I've looked.

Landon Knight II remarked that the horse's name was of the
'genre' of Damon Runyon, implying that there may have been
no specific character called Benny The Dip. If so, it was clever
of Knight to have invented him, but perhaps he didn't.

When *A Very Honorable Guy* was turned into a film in 1934,
Benny appeared played by Hobart Cavanaugh and some cast lists
refer to him as Benny The Dip. So that might be the answer.

There is a Benny The Dip in the 1951 film *St Benny The Dip.*
Benny is played by Dick Haymes, who wasn't a great actor but
was outstanding at getting married, doing so six times, once to
Rita Hayworth.

True to his name, Benny The Dip is a pickpocket, but the film wasn't based on anything written by Damon Runyon but on a story by George Auerbach. Benny is one of three crooks who find refuge and redemption in the Clover Street Mission. Benny pursues Linda Kovacs (Nina Foch), a failed singer and dancer. She then pursues him. All ends well.

> Linda: 'What are you afraid of, Benny?'
> Benny The Dip: 'Old age, the atom bomb …
> also inquisitive dames.'
> *St Benny The Dip, 1951*

Races won: five races, notably the 1996 Group 2 Royal Lodge Stakes and 1997 Group 2 Dante Stakes, not forgetting the Derby.

LEMON DROP KID (1996)
• Kingmambo • Charming Lassie (Seattle Slew)

Unlike Benny The Dip, Lemon Drop Kid was definitely named after a character in a short story by Damon Runyon … except he wasn't. There was certainly a short story by Runyon entitled 'The Lemon Drop Kid' and an earlier *Lemon Drop Kid* (1979) may have been named after him but the multiple Grade 1 winner wasn't.

'The Lemon Drop Kid: A story of the race tracks' first appeared in *Collier's Weekly* in February 1934. Within eight months it had been turned into a film of the same name, reprised in 1951. Yet the 1999 Belmont Stakes and Travers Stakes winner was not named after either the short story or the films.

As a yearling he was bought by Jeanne Vance for $200,000. She had once showed saddle horses and named her acquisition after a multiple world champion harness show horse of the 1950s called Lemon Drop Kid. That Lemon Drop Kid made such an impact that on 11 November 1957 he achieved the rare distinction of appearing on the cover of *Sports Illustrated*.

So now you know.

I am going to take you back a matter of four or five years ago to an August afternoon and the race track at Saratoga and also to a young guy by the name of The Lemon Drop Kid, who is called The Lemon Drop Kid because he always has a little sack of lemon drops in the side pocket of his coat, and is always munching at same.
Opening of 'The Lemon Drop Kid', Collier's Weekly,
3 February 1934

I used to show saddle horses and there was this champion harness horse, Lemon Drop Kid. When it came time to name this horse, I chose that name. Since that time I learned it was a Damon Runyon character.
Jeanne Dance after Lemon Drop Kid won the
1999 Belmont Stakes

Races won: ten in total between 1998 and 2000, including five Grade 1 races, the 1998 Futurity Stakes, 1999 Belmont Stakes and Travers Stakes, 2000 Whitney Handicap and Woodward Stakes.

Half-decent names

Inflexiball (2012)
• Refuse To Bend • Sphere (Daylami)
Won two races in 2017. It's not a lot but it's two more than most horses win. Depressing, isn't it?

Final Straw (1977)
• Thatch • Last Call (Klairon)
Won five races in 1979 and 1980, including the then Group 3 1979 July Stakes.

**BLACK SAM BELLAMY
(NOT FORGETTING GALILEO) (1999)**
• Sadler's Wells • Urban Sea (Miswaki)

What did Galileo and an eighteenth-century pirate called Black
Sam Bellamy have in common? Despite being born over 100 years
apart, they were brothers, their father being Sadler's Wells and
their mother Urban Sea.

Galileo did better, both as a person and a horse. While most
people are only good at one thing or no things, Galileo (1564–
1642) was brilliant at all sorts of things. An inventor, scientist,
astronomer and engineer, after a bit of practice Galileo did just as
well as a racehorse and then a stallion.

There were a few dummy runs, with Galileos foaled in Britain
(1975), France (1993) and Poland (1996). The latter won the 2002
Grade 1 Royal & SunAlliance Novices' Hurdle at Cheltenham
but the genius got into full stride when popping out in Ireland
in 1998. In 2001 Galileo added the Derby, Irish Derby and King
George VI and Queen Elizabeth Diamond Stakes to his long list
of accomplishments before proceeding to establish himself as
a champion sire.

His younger brother was a more dubious character. Samuel
Bellamy (1689–1717) flourished briefly as a pirate, his fortune based
on his capture of the treasure-laden ship the *Whydah* and many
others. More agreeable and less murderous than most pirates,
Black Sam Bellamy avoided the usual fate of capture and execution
but only by going down with the *Whydah* in a storm.

The wreck of the ship was found in 1984 and some of its
valuable contents were recovered. Black Sam Bellamy himself made
a comeback in 1999 and although failing to match his brother's
achievements won a Group 1 race in Italy in 2002 and the Group 1
Tattersalls Gold Cup at the Curragh the following year.

Damn you, you are a sneaking puppy, and so are all those who will submit to be governed by laws which rich men have made for their own security.
Black Sam Bellamy

Skull and crossbones

Shivermetimbers (2012)
• Black Sam Bellamy • Kimouna (Round Sovereign)
Won a bumper race in his first year racing, 2017.

Perfect Pirate (2012)
• Black Sam Bellamy • Supreme Gem (Supreme Leader)
Won a hurdle and a chase for trainer Ben Pauling in 2016 and 2017, with more threatening to come.

Black Pirate (2012)
• Black Sam Bellamy • Proper Posh (Rakaposhi King)
Plundered two bumper races early in 2018, having plundered a point-to-point on his sole previous run, in 2016. Have to hope he doesn't sink like his sire.

Sail With Sultana (2011)
• Black Sam Bellamy • Strathtay (Pivotal)
Sultana was the name of one of the first ships Black Sam Bellamy captured and captained. Sail With Sultana won once from 17 tries – a Flat race at Chepstow in 2015.

BRIGADIER GERARD (1968)
• Queen's Hussar • La Paiva (Prince Chevalier)

Sherlock Holmes wasn't Arthur Conan Doyle's only popular creation. Professor Challenger and Brigadier Gerard also had their followers.

Brigadier Etienne Gerard was the comically vain yet brave hero of a string of short stories that appeared originally in the *Strand* magazine, largely between 1894 and 1903. Both the human and equine Brigadier Gerard were hussars, the horse being by Queen's Hussar while Conan Doyle's character was a hussar in Napoleon's army.

In Brigadier Gerard's opinion, medals awarded to him were well deserved and those not awarded were also deserved. Etienne believed that if he had not been unavoidably absent from the Battle of Waterloo, the outcome might have been different.

There was less doubt about the horse's achievements. Brigadier Gerard is one of horseracing's greatest champions. Bred and owned by John and Jean Hislop, Brigadier Gerard had every quality required of a champion, in abundance. Physically impressive, he repeatedly proved himself to have not just brilliance and class but also soundness, courage, enthusiasm, resilience and versatility. At the highest level he took on every challenge and was beaten only once in 18 races, by Roberto in the 1972 Benson and Hedges Gold Cup at York.

Today you can either watch him on YouTube or toast him at the Brigadier Gerard pub in Horton Heath, Hampshire.

> You cannot see the lettuce and the dressing
> without suspecting a salad.
> 'How the Brigadier was Tempted by the Devil' in *The Exploits of Brigadier Gerard* (1896)

Races won: 1970 Middle Park Stakes; 1971 2,000 Guineas, St James's Palace Stakes, Sussex Stakes, Queen Elizabeth II Stakes, Champion Stakes; 1972 Lockinge Stakes, Prince of Wales's Stakes, Eclipse Stakes, King George VI and Queen Elizabeth Stakes, Queen Elizabeth II Stakes, Champion Stakes; plus five other races. Not bad, eh?

Bad names

Aerosol (1974)

• Great Nephew • Psalmodie (Nasram)

What sort of name is that for a noble thoroughbred? Amazingly, he won a Group 3 race at Saint-Cloud in 1976.

Aerosol (2009)

• Public Purse • Nina Sabella (Jules)

What sort of name is that for a noble thoroughbred? Amazingly, the Brazilian-bred colt won two Group 1 races in Rio de Janeiro in 2013. It just goes to show.

CALIGULA (1917)
• The Tetrarch • Snoot (Perigord)

The Roman emperor (from AD 37 to 41) may not have been as murderous, lecherous, sadistic and insane as dubious history relates but he was pretty awful, eventually assassinated and an unlikely winner of the St Leger.

At least Caligula was keen on horseracing and reputedly fed his favourite horse, Incitatus, on oats mixed with gold flakes served in an ivory manger. Caligula considered making Incitatus a consul but settled for making him a priest; so it was said.

In 1918 the 6th Earl of Wilton bought Caligula as a yearling for 8,100 guineas (equal to £500,000 today, depending on which unreliable method you opt for). Two years later Caligula, who had won the Ascot Derby (later renamed the King Edward

VII Stakes), was considered good enough to run in the St Leger. Unfortunately, Lord Wilton's financial situation presented an ill-timed obstacle related to the fact that, as one newspaper reported, he was 'considered to be the heaviest plunger [gambler] on the English Turf'.

A few days before the race, Wilton was the subject of a court order preventing him from running Caligula unless the horse was sold. Mathradas Goculdas, an Indian textile magnate, obliged for 8,000 guineas, with half the prize money going to Wilton should Caligula win. He did, at 100-6.

For Wilton it was a temporary reprieve. Two months later, Alexander Ross-Hume obtained a divorce from his wife Mabel on the grounds of 'her misconduct with the Earl of Wilton'. While Mabel was staying with her brother, Robert Sievier junior, Wilton was a regular visitor. Sievier's butler, Cuthbert Samson, testified that when he took tea and the post to the lady's bedroom, the door was often opened by Lord Wilton. After divorce papers were served Wilton, as Mrs Ross-Hume stated, 'ran away and left me to face the publicity and unhappiness alone'.

Lord Wilton died in 1927, aged 31. Caligula proved infertile at stud.

> I realised what sort of man I had loved and trusted and what a ghastly mistake I had made.
> *Mrs Ross-Hume of Lord Wilton, 1920*

Races won: 1920 Ascot Derby and St Leger, plus one other race.

Splendid names

Bachelors Pad (1994)

• Pursuit Of Love • Note Book (Mummy's Pet)
Won nine races on the Flat and over hurdles between 1996 and 2002, six of them selling or claiming races.

The Gatting Ball (2014)
• Hard Spun • Art Of Deception (Artie Schiller)
Otherwise known in cricketing circles, particularly Australian ones, as 'the ball of the century'.

It was Shane Warne's first delivery on his first appearance in the first match of the 1993 Ashes series at Old Trafford. The ball bounced outside the leg stump, spun sharply past Mike Gatting's bat and removed the bail from his off stump.

As a horse, The Gatting Ball has yet to strike in nine attempts in 2017 and 2018 in Australia.

CAPTAIN CEE BEE (2001)
• Germany • Elea Victoria (Sharp Victor)

In 2001 Eddie Harty bought a foal for IR4,500 guineas. Harty, who rode Highland Wedding to victory in the 1969 Grand National, thought well of the colt because he named him after his father, Captain Cyril Bold Harty.

In the early 1920s, Captain Harty was an officer in the Free State Army. In 1926 he was one of the pioneers in a hastily prepared three-man team representing the Irish Army at the Royal Dublin Society's Horse Show. It was an impressive achievement to finish runner-up to Switzerland, ahead of teams from Britain, France, Holland and Belgium. *An-t-Oglach* (the *Army Journal*), stated that it wished to 'compliment Capt. Cyril Bold Harty on his great success at the recent Horse Show in Dublin'.

Two years later Harty was a member of the team that won the Nations' Cup, and he went on to train Knight's Crest to win the 1944 Irish Grand National.

The Captain's grandson, Eddie Harty junior, trained Captain Cee Bee to win a bumper race and a maiden race on the Flat, after which the six-year-old was sold to JP McManus but remained with Harty. Captain Cee Bee was the versatile, enduring kingpin of the yard, racing from 2005 to 2014, his career highlighted by victory in the

2008 Supreme Novices' Hurdle at the Cheltenham Festival. Even as a 13-year-old Captain Cee Bee was capable of decent performances.

> When I die I'm going to leave my money to my daughters and to you I will leave my eye for a horse for you to make a living.
> *Captain Cyril Bold Harty to his three sons. I expect they'd have preferred the money.*

Races won: 13 from 36 appearances. As well as the Supreme Novices' Hurdle, Captain Cee Bee won the Grade 1 Ryanair Novice Chase at Punchestown in 2010 and two Grade 2 hurdles, once when aged 12.

CARAVAGGIO (2014)
• Scat Daddy • Mekko Hokte (Holy Bull)

Luckily, Caravaggio the racehorse, trained by Aidan O'Brien, shared the winning talent of his artist namesake without his violent tendencies.

Regarded as one of the most influential painters of his time but argumentative and difficult, Caravaggio (1571–1610) was prone to brawling. After a fight in Milan in 1592 he left for Rome where, in 1606, he killed someone, possibly without intending to, and was sentenced to death. From Rome he fled to Naples, was imprisoned in 1608 after more brawling, and escaped only to be attacked and injured. Seeking a Papal pardon for the earlier unfortunate murder, Caravaggio died in 1610 en route to Rome. It was amazing that he found time to paint.

> All works, no matter what or by whom painted, are nothing but bagatelles and childish trifles unless they are made and painted from life.
> *Caravaggio (the artist)*

He's the fastest we've ever had.
*Aidan O'Brien, although he may have said something
similar before.*

Races won: seven, notably the 2016 Group 2 Coventry Stakes and
Group 1 Phoenix Stakes; 2017 Group 1 Commonwealth Cup
and Group 2 Flying Five Stakes.

Dreadful name

Discount Cycles (1974)
● Sovereign Gleam ● Debatable (Counsel)
A marketing inspiration, I expect. Hopeless in 1976 and again in 1977.

Another dreadful name

Estate Agent (1973)
● Candy Cane ● Creel Inn (Premonition)
Granted, owner George Leatham was an estate agent, and it could
have been worse – he might have been a sewer cleaner. Estate Agent
won a Flat race in 1973, two hurdle races in 1977 and 1978 and
a chase in 1981.

CLYDE VAN DUSEN (1926)
● Man O'War ● Uncle's Lassie (Uncle)

Uniquely, Clyde Van Dusen won a Kentucky Derby both as a horse
and a trainer. Both were small – Van Dusen had been a jockey – and
that was why owner Herbert Gardner, who had a broom factory in
Amsterdam, named his horse after his trainer.

The 1929 Kentucky Derby was run in a mudbath, which was
fortunate for Clyde Van Dusen, who wore mud caulks, but not for
the favourite, Blue Larkspur, who didn't. Colonel Edward Bradley

(see section 5), the owner of Blue Larkspur, was not impressed. In a fit of pique, he suggested that Clyde Van Dusen was 'the worst horse to win the Derby in 20 years'.

There were several unique features about that year's Run for the Roses. It was the last to be started from a web barrier rather than starting gates and the trophy has disappeared. If you know where it is please let Churchill Downs racetrack know.

> I was kinda scared when I first saw Clyde because he is so little but, oh boy, how he can run! He is nothing but a mud-runnin' fool!
> *Winning jockey Linus 'Pony' McAtee*

Races won: a dozen in all, including the 1928 Kentucky Jockey Club Stakes and, obviously, the 1929 Kentucky Derby.

DANCING BRAVE (1983)
• Lyphard • Navajo Princess (Drone)

I'm guessing that trainer Guy Harwood's and owner Prince Khalid Abdullah's champion was so-called because his dam was Navajo Princess. The seminal race in his career was the 1986 Derby.

There are two opinions about the ride Greville Starkey gave Dancing Brave. One is that Starkey, riding a waiting race, was beaten by an unhelpful drop in pace at a crucial stage, leaving him with too much ground to make up. The second is that Starkey made a complete balls-up of it, giving away far too much ground and leaving Dancing Brave with an impossible task which the horse's brilliance almost overcame. The second opinion is the correct one. Shahrastani (see section 15) won by half a length.

Under Pat Eddery, Dancing Brave went on to win the King George VI and Queen Elizabeth Diamond Stakes and Prix de l'Arc de Triomphe in scintillating style, to be celebrated as an equine great.

You won't see him until late.
Pat Eddery before the Arc

When I finally pulled him out, Dancing Brave was electrifying. Boy, did he go. I have never felt anything like it.
Pat Eddery after the Arc

Races won: 1986 2,000 Guineas, Coral-Eclipse Stakes, King George VI and Queen Elizabeth Diamond Stakes, Prix de l'Arc de Triomphe and four others.

> **A good name**
>
> **Class Act (1986)**
> • Shirley Heights • Thespian (Ile de Bourbon)
> Shirley Heights won the 1978 Derby. You can work out the rest for yourself.
> Class Act wasn't one, winning just two minor races in 1990.

DESERT ORCHID (1979)
• Grey Mirage • Flower Child (Brother)

A charismatic grey who took on fences with daring elan and enthusiasm, Desert Orchid attracted a degree of admiration and affection that very few horses have received or deserved. People loved him.

Although it might be assumed that Desert Orchid's name stemmed from those of his parents, owner-breeders James and Midge Burridge and their son Richard originally planned to call him Desert Air, after a line in Thomas Gray's poem 'Elegy Written in a Country Churchyard' (1751).

The name was available but Weatherbys objected because there was already a horse racing under the name of Desert Heir. If they ever ran in the same race it would have been a commentator's nightmare. The Burridges decided to keep the Desert and add Orchid after Grey Orchid, Flower Child's dam. It's best that you know, as it may come up in a quiz.

Prone to treat hurdles with a cavalier disdain that sometimes resulted in disaster, Desert Orchid sailed over fences with a fearless, spectacular zeal that was bliss for photographers and exhilarating for race fans.

Widely considered to be best over two miles, the minimum distance in jumps races, Desert Orchid confounded many by winning the 1988 Whitbread Gold Cup over three miles five furlongs before putting up a tremendously gutsy performance to win the 1989 Cheltenham Gold Cup in conditions that tested resolve as well as stamina.

Desert Orchid was everything that could be dreamt of in a steeplechaser, a dream come true for owners the Burridges, trainer David Elsworth and followers of racing. He died in 2006, aged 27; his ashes were buried at Kempton racecourse, where Desert Orchid had won the King George VI Chase four times.

> He was simply the most complete racehorse I ever sat on.
> His greatest attributes were his courage and his jumping.
> *Simon Sherwood, who rode Desert Orchid when he won the*
> *Cheltenham Gold Cup and in two of his four victories in the*
> *King George VI Chase*

Races won: 34 from 71 appearances between 1983 and 1991, including 1986 King George VI Chase; 1988 Whitbread Gold Cup, Tingle Creek Chase, King George VI Chase; 1989 Victor Chandler Chase, Cheltenham Gold Cup, King George VI Chase; 1990 Racing Post Chase, Irish Grand National, King George VI Chase.

DICK TURPIN (2007)
• Arakan • Merrily (Sharrood)

In folklore a romantic highwayman but in reality a murderous thief with no redeeming qualities, Dick Turpin's sole acquaintanceship with the Knavesmire at York was when hanged there in 1739, aged 33.

Unsurprisingly, Dick Turpin (equine variety) was beaten on his only appearance at York, in the 2010 Juddmonte International but he deserved to be there, having recently won the Group 1 Prix Jean Prat at Chantilly and been runner-up in the Group 1 St James's Palace Stakes at Royal Ascot.

Trained by Richard Hannon senior, Dick Turpin won nine times between 2009 and 2011, and when he didn't win he often finished second, as in the 2010 2,000 Guineas.

> Three hundred guineas on Turpin's head,
> Trap him alive or shoot him dead.
> *From* The Ballad of Dick Turpin *by Alfred Noyes*

Races won: six Group races, including 2010 Group 1 Prix Jean Prat and 2011 Group 1 Premio Vittorio Di Capua.

BLACK BESS (2013)
• Dick Turpin • Spring Clean (Danehill)

Fittingly, Dick Turpin sired Black Bess, an imaginary creature in the highwayman's tale that is reputed to have carried Turpin from London to York in record time before, understandably, dropping dead. Black Bess did better as a racehorse, winning six times for trainer Jim Boyle between 2016 and 2018.

> From the West was her dam; from the East her sire.
> From the one came her swiftness; the other her fire.
> No peer of the realm better blood can possess

Than flows in the blood of my bonny Black Bess.
Epitaph for Black Bess

Part 2

It's no different from Part 1. I just thought the section was too long and it might seem shorter this way.

FRANKEL (2008)
 • Galileo • Kind (Danehill)

Frankel was an incomparable racehorse and a gripping story rolled into one.

Bobby Frankel was Prince Khalid Abdullah's trainer in the USA. Shortly after Frankel succumbed to leukaemia, in November 2009, a yearling by Galileo out of Kind was named Frankel in his honour and sent to be trained in Britain by Henry Cecil.

Frankel's unmatched achievements on the track – between August 2010 and October 2012 he was unbeaten in 14 races including ten Group 1 events – formed part of a picture in which Cecil and Bobby Frankel were drawn together.

Born into different worlds – Frankel a brash Brooklyn Jew from a humble background, Cecil a quietly spoken figure from a distinguished military and aristocratic family – the two had more than Khalid Abdullah and racehorses in common. Both were fiercely competitive – Frankel overtly, Cecil less obviously. There was domestic turmoil in both their lives and their late careers were shadowed by cancer.

Bobby Frankel died nine months before his namesake made his debut, while Cecil died eight months after his champion's final appearance. Increasingly gaunt and ravaged, Cecil seemed to be kept alive by Frankel, the trainer determined not to miss a single one of the great horse's races.

He's the best I've ever had, the best I've ever seen.
I'd be very surprised if there's ever been better.
*Henry Cecil after Frankel's final victory in the 2012
Champion Stakes*

Races won: 2010 Dewhurst Stakes and three other races; 2011 2,000
Guineas, St James's Palace Stakes, Sussex Stakes, Queen Elizabeth
II Stakes and one other race; 2012 Lockinge Stakes, Queen Anne
Stakes, Sussex Stakes, Juddmonte International, Champion Stakes.

Not bad

Goody Goody (1978)
• Mummy's Pet • Righteous Girl (Right Boy)
Won once.

Hypodermic (1977)
• Steel Heart • Narcotic (Narrator)
Won once.

Final Call (1978)
• Town Crier • Last Case (Firestreak)
Won once. Well, it's better than not once.

GHOFAR (1983)
• Nicholas Bill • Royale Final (Henry The Seventh)

In 2000 John Randall, a racing historian and statistician who
worked for the *Racing Post*, won £500,000 on *Who Wants to Be
a Millionaire?* He knew what most people didn't, that a spelunker
is someone who explores caves.

After big wins, winners often say that it won't change their lives
but that is rarely true. If it's been true of anyone, it will have been
true of Randall. He will have carried on living the life he already

lived, because he is not someone for whom the trappings of wealth hold much appeal.

Nor does he allow sentiment to influence his assessment of a racehorse's merit. So when Randall placed Ghofar 'at the very bottom' of the list of Hennessy Gold Cup winners (*Racing Post*, 28 November 2002), only a brave man would challenge him.

The half-owner of Ghofar, Sir Hugh Dundas (1920–95), was the bravest of men. In 1988, the year before Ghofar's Hennessy triumph, Dundas's *Flying Start: A Fighter Pilot's War Years* was published. It told the story of a young Spitfire pilot's struggle to reconcile his 'sincere desire to engage the enemy' with his 'sincere desire to stay alive' when it was difficult to do both.

Aged 19, he was being shot at by Messerschmitts; at 20 he was shot down twice. 'Death stretched out its hand to touch me every day,' he wrote. 'Everybody was frightened and everybody knew that everybody else was frightened.' Dundas felt fear but faced it down.

In 1940 his brother John, also a pilot, was killed. During a two-month period in 1941, Dundas's squadron lost half its pilots. That year, Dundas was awarded the Distinguished Flying Cross and, aged 21, became Squadron Leader. A year later, he was promoted to Wing Commander, and in 1944 was awarded the Distinguished Service Order. Aged 24, he became the youngest ever Group Captain.

After the war, Dundas held exalted posts in the media, including latterly as chairman of Thames Television. He was married to Lord Oaksey's sister, Enid Rosamond Lawrence.

> Oberon is the satellite of which planet?
> If John Randall had known that the answer was Uranus
> he'd have won £1 million.

Races won: between 1986 and 1994 Ghofar won two hurdle races and eight chases; not bad for a horse that cost 1,000 guineas as a yearling.

GIMCRACK (1760)
• Cripple • Miss Elliott (Partner)

Here's a funny thing (see Max Miller in section 7). The Gimcrack
Stakes is a major race for two-year-olds run over six furlongs at York
in August. It has been run there since 1846, yet Gimcrack didn't run
as a two-year-old, never ran over six furlongs – he often ran over four
miles – and was beaten on his two appearances at York.

The oddity is explained by his ability and popularity. In a long
racing career, from 1764 to 1771, Gimcrack, a notably small grey, won
27 of his 36 races and attracted an enthusiastic following. In 1770
a group of admirers in York founded the Gimcrack Club and in 1846
launched the Gimcrack Stakes. Traditionally, each December the
winning owner delivers a speech at the Gimcrack Club dinner.

> There was a meeting of two days at Newmarket this time
> of year, to see the sweetest little horse run that ever was;
> his name is Gimcrack, he is delightful.
> *Lady Sarah Bunbury, writing in July 1765*

Races won: I shouldn't need to tell you twice: see above.

HANDICAPPER (1898)
• Matchmaker • Agnes Osborne (Beaudesert)

Handicappers don't win Classics and Handicapper was just
a handicapper, who started at 33-1 for the 1901 2,000 Guineas.
Appropriately, in his previous race two weeks earlier, Handicapper
was unplaced, at 100-8, in a handicap. Owner Sir Ernest Cassel
didn't bother to go to Newmarket for the Guineas. He should have
done, because to the delight of jockey Bill Halsey and trainer Fred
Day but the horror of almost everyone else, Handicapper won.

'Magpie' in the *Globe* was appalled by the result, and perhaps
had suffered himself. 'The astounding result was a severe financial
blow to speculators,' he wrote. 'Handicapper's success caused

utter rout to everybody, he being clearly inferior to quite half of the field.'

He won, though, and unlike any other Classic winner you care to name, Handicapper was the first horse to win a Classic in a race started by gate. My case rests.

> There could have been no possible ground for espousing the claims of Handicapper who is evidently more than his name might suggest.
> Globe, *2 May 1901*

Races won: 1901 2,000 Guineas.

A likeable name

Drama Critic (1974)
• Reviewer • Sophist (Acropolis)
The owner may not have rated drama critics highly but this one won ten times in the USA, including the prestigious Ramona Handicap at Del Mar in 1978.

J J THE JET PLANE (2004)
• Jet Master • Majestic Guest (Northern Guest)

Named, unless I'm mistaken, after *Jay Jay The Jet Plane* (too many letters), a children's television programme featuring Tarrytown Airport and its aeroplanes, notably a small blue jet called Jay Jay.

South Africa's great sprinter, sold for a desperate R15,000 (£1,300) as a foal and for only R70,000 (£5,700) as a two-year-old, dominated South Africa's top sprints between 2008 and 2010, during which J J The Jet Plane won six Grade 1 events in South Africa.

The prize money was low compared to that for big international races and at the end of 2010 J J The Jet Plane's career and profile reached a new level when, trained by Lucky Houdalakis, the six-

year-old won the Group 1 Hong Kong Sprint and HK$7,980,000
(£635,000). The previous year, when temporarily trained by Mike
de Kock, J J The Jet Plane had won what was then the Group 3
Al Quoz Sprint at Nad Al Sheba. In 2011 J J The Jet Plane won the
same race, by then a Group 2 event at the new Meydan racecourse.

> The sun is rising high up over Tarrytown,
> Friends taking off and friends touching down.
> That's where you'll find,
> That one of a kind.
> Jay Jay
> Jay Jay the Jet Plane!
> *Theme song by Parachute Express*

Races won: 14 in all between 2007 and 2012. If you'd been
paying attention you'd already know which were the important ones.

JIMMY THE JETPLANE (2008)
• Jimble • C'est Cool (Roi Guillaume)

Not quite in the same class but a very decent hurdler and chaser who,
so far, has won six times under Rules, latterly when ridden in hunter
chases by his splendidly named owner, Mr James Jackson-Stops.
Jackson-Stops is perhaps related to Jackson-Stops, a large estate agents
well placed to put several houses on a Jackson-Stops mount.

JUDGE HIMES (1900)
• Esher • Lullaby (Longfellow)

Even though the field for the 1903 Kentucky Derby was a weak one,
few believed it was weak enough to give Judge Himes a chance of
winning. His jockey, Hal Booker, said afterwards, 'I did not think
I had a chance to win the race when I started.'

As a two-year-old, Judge Himes, named after Judge Isodore
Himes, a friend of owner Charles 'The Blond Plunger' Ellison,

had won only one of his seven races. In 1903 he had been unplaced in all three of his pre-Kentucky Derby runs.

The odds-on favourite was Early, ridden by the black jockey Jimmy Winkfield, going for a hat-trick of Kentucky Derby wins. Early was making his seasonal debut and lacked conditioning, but Winkfield rode a poor race, as he himself admitted, making his run too soon.

In subsequent years, Ellison's gambling fortunes rose and fell dizzily. In 1911 connections of Governor Gray, the beaten Kentucky Derby favourite, believed that Roscoe Troxler, Governor Gray's jockey, had pulled the horse and that Ellison was involved.

The day after the race, Ellison was allegedly seen handing Troxler money. Governor Gray's owner, Captain Jim Williams, later attacked Ellison with a heavy cane but accusations of race-fixing were not proved.

As soon as I got up on equal terms with Early, Winkfield turned around at me and laughed. It was then that I was sure that I did not have a chance. That ******, I was sure, was trying to make a sucker out of me.
Winning jockey Hal Booker. Shockingly to modern ears and eyes, Booker twice used a racist term when referring to Winkfield and the newspapers printed it. Courier-Journal, *3 May 1903*

Mullaney, all I am sorry for is that I can't sentence you to be publicly whipped. The whipping post for wife-beaters is the only effective remedy. If I had the authority to sentence you to be flogged, I would certainly do so.
Judge Isadore Himes in a Chicago court. He fined Charles Mullaney, a violent drunkard who regularly assaulted his wife Maria, £20 plus costs. As Mullaney couldn't pay he was sent to prison. Greensboro Daily News, *17 April 1907*

Races won: 18 from 104 appearances, mainly in minor races well after his shock success in the 1903 Kentucky Derby.

KYBO (1973)
* Candy Cane • Viquest (Vimy)

Isidore Kerman was, among several other occupations, a solicitor active in the divorce market. In the 1930s one of his clients was the former champion Flat jockey and multiple Classic race winner Tommy Weston. When it came to the fee, Weston offered payment in the form of a yearling. Kerman accepted.

He named the colt Kybo, after his mother's advice when a schoolboy to 'Keep Your Bowels Open', in 1937, Kybo won a race for two-year-olds at Manchester, ridden by Weston.

At the same time, Kerman had a good greyhound named Brilliant Kybo and 40 years later resurrected Kybo in improved form as a jumper.

It would be exaggerating to say that Kybo was a celebrated champion but he was second favourite for the Champion Hurdle in 1979 and trainer Josh Gifford was convinced that he would have beaten Monksfield but for falling at the second last hurdle. As it was, Kybo won several prestigious hurdle races.

Kerman also won the 1961 Ascot Stakes with Angazi and in the same year bought Plumpton racecourse. In 1970 he bought Fontwell Park. On his death in 1998, aged 93, Kerman still owned both, although he had given up riding when 86. People give up too easily when they get older.

Races won: Ten hurdle races, including the 1977 Black and White Whisky Hurdle and SGB Hurdle, 1978 Kirk and Kirk Hurdle, SGB Hurdle and Christmas Hurdle. Also won four chases.

A splendid name

Bungee Jumper (1990)
* Idiots Delight • Catherine Bridge (Pitpan)
Won five races, appropriately over jumps, between 1994 and 2003.

MARQUIS DE SADE (1973)
• Queen's Hussar • Sweet Charity (Javelot)

Many people have had horses named after them but few have had words named after them, especially words like 'sadism' and 'sadist'.

It was probably for the best that the notorious Marquis de Sade (1740–1814) spent half his adult life in either prisons or asylums. Although the French aristocrat wasn't officially declared insane until 1803, he had regularly behaved like a madman for many years, as countless victims of his sexual extremism could testify.

When de Sade wasn't indulging in sexual abuse, he was writing about it at great length, including in the landmark work *Les 120 Journées de Sodome*, written in the 1780s during a spell in the Bastille. De Sade was not a good role model, his behaviour often being 'inappropriate'. He was better behaved on racecourses, winning the 1976 King Edward VII Stakes at Royal Ascot for owner Charles St George, himself prone to controversy.

> The most impure tale that has ever been told since the world began.
> *The Marquis de Sade's stated vision for* Les 120 Journées de Sodome: *an ambition fulfilled.*

Races won: 1976 King Edward VII Stakes and two other races.

Jolly good names

Regency Brighton (1978)
• Royal Palace • Gay City (Forlorn River)
Like so many, a non-winner.

One Fleet Street (1977)
• Habitat • The Creditor (Crepello)
1 Fleet Street is the address of Child & Co., a bank that now forms part of the Royal Bank of Scotland. The horse won five times.

Lone Bidder (1978)
- Auction Ring • Seul (Faberge)
Won twice, including a Group 3 race in Ireland.

POSSE (1977)
• Forli • In Hot Pursuit (Bold Ruler)

As Posse's dam was called In Hot Pursuit, Posse was
quite well named, as was his owner, Ogden Mills Phipps,
a wealthy American financier and leading figure in the racing
and breeding industry.

In 1980 Posse, trained by John Dunlop, won the St James's
Palace Stakes and Sussex Stakes and was the moral victor in the
2,000 Guineas, although the heartless record book ascribes victory
to Known Fact.

For those who backed Posse at 12-1 – I am thinking particularly
of me – the race was torment and its recollection painful. To quote
Timeform's *Racehorses of 1980*, 'Posse suffered wretched luck in
the race, being almost brought down by Nureyev more than two
furlongs out. Posse recovered an enormous amount of ground to
finish third, a neck and three-quarters of a length behind Nureyev
and Known Fact.'

Nureyev was disqualified and Posse promoted to second place
but it was one more reason to develop an aversion to Newmarket's
Rowley Mile. I suppose it's time to forget about it. I still don't like
the Rowley Mile.

Posse was a much underrated colt who should have
won the 2,000 Guineas.
John Dunlop in 2005. Hear hear.

Races won: 1980 St James's Palace Stakes and Sussex Stakes.

Eat Cake (1988)
• Legend of France • Guillotina (Busted)
Perhaps the filly acted on her name and found it disagreed with her –
she never raced.

Let Them Eat Cake (2007)
• Danehill Dancer • Lady Adnil (Stravinsky)
The dismissive comment reputedly but probably not uttered by Marie
Antoinette on being told that peasants had no bread and were starving.
Let Them Eat Cake ran only three times, poorly.

RADIOTHERAPY (1943)
• Hyperion • Belleva (Stratford)

It's a strange name to give a horse but not as strange as the life of the
owner's wife, Mrs Vera Lilley, formerly Mrs Cottingham, before that
Mrs Owen, before that Miss Sklarevskia, latterly Mrs Hue-Williams.

Radiotherapy was well chosen as he won the 1946 Sussex
Stakes and finished third in that year's Derby. Vera's husbands
were well chosen, too, the final three all being multi-
millionaires, while the first, George Owen, a British diplomat,
was soon divorced.

Sklarevskia was born in Kiev in 1899, the daughter of Baroness
Kostovsky, an unhelpful title when the Bolsheviks came to power.
The Baroness and her two daughters fled to Paris with the family
jewels sewn into the hems of their petticoats.

Free of Mr Owen, in 1931 Vera married Walter Sherwin
Cottingham, whose father had conveniently died the previous
year, leaving her new husband over £400,000 (equivalent to
£24 million today) including ownership of Lewis Berger, a major
paint manufacturer. Five years later Walter died, leaving his

widow £217,000 (£14 million). In 1940, Vera moved into shoes
by marrying Thomas Lilley of Lilley & Skinner. Together they set
up studs in England and Ireland and hosted lavish parties. Along
the way, racing in Mrs Lilley's colours, Supreme Court won the
1951 Chester Vase, King Edward VII Stakes and King George VI
and Queen Elizabeth Festival of Britain Stakes.

Thomas died in 1959 and in 1963 Vera married Colonel Roger
Hue-Williams, a wealthy stockbroker and Turfite. Vera had
already won the St Leger with Aurelius in 1961 and ten years later
her husband won the 1,000 Guineas, Oaks and Irish Oaks with
Altesse Royale. In the 1974 Irish Derby, Vera's English Prince beat
Roger's Imperial Prince.

Her final husband died in 1987 and Vera followed five
years later, leaving £9 million (£18 million today), including
£3 million from Christie's sale of 'The Magnificent Jewels of
Vera Hue-Williams'.

Her former initials of V L live on in the entrance gates of
Newtown Stud, which she once owned, while the stud's current
owner, Sheila Grassick, named a horse *Vera Lilley* (2006). Sadly,
she didn't win.

> The top lot of her collection was a large necklace fashioned
> from Burmese rubies, which a European dealer bought for
> $1.1 million.
> *Report of the 1995 sale of Vera Hue-Williams's jewellery*

Races won: 1945 won at Salisbury and Windsor; 1946 Newmarket
Stakes and Sussex Stakes.

PRETTY JEWEL (2013)
• Aqlaam • Highland Jewel (Azamour)

A very different kind of champion and a very different jewel.
Rather than Christie's, it was Tattersalls, and Pretty Jewel
cost Dr Misha Voikhansky just 2,500 guineas. There was

another link. Vera Sklarevskia had fled from the Bolsheviks
and in 1975 Misha's mother, Marina, a psychiatrist, fled
Leonid Brezhnev's Russia after protesting against the abuse
of psychiatry to punish dissidents.

Misha, then aged nine, was not allowed to leave. The playwright
Tom Stoppard, with support from Harold Pinter, Yehudi Menuhin
and Joan Baez, led a Free Misha Campaign. The government urged
Russia to allow Misha to join his mother and in 1979 he was finally
allowed to do so.

Misha qualified as a doctor in 1992 and works as a GP
in a suburb of Birmingham. Finding racing appealing,
Dr Voikhansky was not content to watch; he wanted to race
himself. Aged 50, he had his first ride in 2016 and, a champion
in his way, rode Pretty Jewel to victory at Salisbury in 2017 and
again, aged 52 at Doncaster and Goodwood in 2018. Magnificent!

Good names

Speargun (1974)

• Deep Diver • Annie Oakley (Big Game)
Annie Oakley (1860–1926) was a famous American sharpshooter
whose fame spread through touring with Buffalo Bill's Wild West Show.
Speargun, in contrast, failed to hit the bullseye once.

Suavity (1977)

• Personality • Smooth (Sound Track)
Charmed his way to four successes.

Seven Hearts (1976)

• Some Hand • Vienna Love (Vienna)
Won five races.

RED CANDLE (1964)
• Autumn Gold • Rose Gallica (Rudolpho)

In 1971, David Elsworth, later famous for training Desert Orchid and Persian Punch, arrived at Lieutenant-Colonel 'Ricky' Vallance's stables at Bishops Cannings in Wiltshire with a couple of horses. It was agreed that Vallance would train them and Elsworth ride work but Elsworth soon found himself doing much of the training himself. When Red Candle won the Mackeson Gold Cup in 1972 and the Hennessy Gold Cup the year after, Vallance was the licensed trainer but arguably the credit belonged to Elsworth.

Six months after the Hennessy, Vallance was disqualified for a year when Well Briefed landed a gamble at Devon and Exeter after two recent heavy defeats. The stewards were not satisfied with Vallance's explanation for the horse's sudden improvement.

The eccentric Lieutenant-Colonel went on to lose his trainer's licence once more and his driver's licence twice. Luckily, he had trained Saxon Warrior to carry him home from the Crown pub nearby, although on one occasion, while negotiating the churchyard, Vallance fell into a newly dug grave and had to be pulled out. A sort of dress rehearsal.

> Saturdays are eventful for trainer Ricky Vallance. On November 11th Red Candle won the Mackeson Gold Cup for him at 20-1. Last Saturday Ricky fell off a ladder and broke some ribs.
> Daily Mirror, *1 December 1972. Lieutenant-Colonel Vallance was often in trouble of one kind or another.*

Races won: three hurdles and seven chases between 1970 and 1973.

> ### RED RUM (1965)
> • Quorum • Mared (Magic Red)

Like the Queen, Red Rum is a much loved national treasure, etched into the country's collective consciousness.

Bred in Ireland by Martyn McEnery, Red Rum's name was formed from the last three letters of his dam's and sire's names. Mared, his dam, was generally considered to be mad and Red Rum's pedigree unpromising, so it was not surprising that he was sold as a yearling for only 400 guineas. The following year, the day before Foinavon won the Grand National, Red Rum dead-heated to half-win the five-furlong Thursby Selling Plate at Aintree. At the subsequent auction, owner Maurice Kingsley retained Red Rum for 300 guineas.

What followed was a Cinderella story whose romantic highlights unfolded after Red Rum was bought by trainer Donald 'Ginger' McCain in 1972 for 6,000 guineas to race in the colours of Noel Le Mare.

McCain was then a part-time taxi driver. When Frank Sinatra was performing in Blackpool, McCain chauffeured him around the town in search of a hairbrush. According to McCain, Sinatra didn't give him a tip. Perhaps McCain had previously given Sinatra one. Le Mare, already 84 in 1972, was a more regular customer.

Regularly exercised on the beach at Southport as a treatment for a bone disease in his feet, Red Rum was the villain in the 1973 Grand National, seizing victory from the magnificent Crisp, who carried 12st to Red Rum's 10st 5lb. The next year Red Rum was the hero, himself defying 12st and going on to win the Scottish Grand National under 11st 13lb.

In those days the Aintree fences were more formidable than today. Red Rum was not a big horse but he was beautifully balanced, a nimble and economical jumper who, in 100 jumps races, never fell.

Remarkably, Red Rum then finished runner-up in both the 1975 and 1976 Nationals, to L'Escargot and Rag Trade respectively.

To seal the fairytale, in 1977, aged 12, he won for a third time. His achievement will never be matched.

Red Rum enjoyed a long, active retirement, celebrated wherever he went. He died in 1995, aged 30, and was buried near Aintree's winning post.

> He's coming up to the line to win it like a fresh horse.
> *Peter O'Sullevan's memorable, if questionable, comment*
> *at the end of the four-mile-plus 1977 Grand National*

Races won: three on the Flat and 24 over jumps between 1967 and 1978, including the 1973, 1974 and 1977 Grand Nationals.

SHERGAR (1978)
• Great Nephew • Sharmeen (Val De Loir)

Shergar had two claims to fame, the first desirable, the second fatal.

A big-girthed chestnut colt with a striking white blaze and a quick, scuttling action, Shergar rose imperiously above his contemporaries and laid claim to be one of the all-time greats.

As a three-year-old, having won the Sandown Classic Trial by ten lengths and the Chester Vase by a dozen lengths, Shergar outclassed his Derby rivals to win by an unprecedented ten lengths, eased down. To add to the occasion, the Aga Khan-owned, Michael Stoute-trained winner was ridden by Walter Swinburn, aged just 19.

Shergar followed up by winning the Irish Derby and King George VI and Queen Elizabeth Diamond Stakes before his magical run came to an end in the St Leger. At the end of 1981 the Aga Khan's champion was retired to the Ballymany Stud in Ireland.

In February 1983, Shergar was kidnapped by the IRA, who demanded a ransom of £2 million. The Aga Khan was no longer the stallion's sole owner. Shergar had been valued at £10 million (about £39 million today), with the Aga Khan retaining six of the 40 shares. The horse's multiple ownership complicated negotiations and either because the IRA lost patience with the negotiations or, more likely, the horse had been injured, Shergar was shot.

> On Derby Day, Shergar was very special. Once Walter pressed the button, the race was over so quickly, he was so dynamic.
> *Michael Stoute reflecting on the 1981 Derby*

> Every day, I would see him first thing in the morning, when I fed him, and last thing at night. He was a grand horse, a nice horse, with a lovely temperament.
> *Jim Fitzgerald, head groom at Ballymany Stud*

Races won: six, notably the 1981 Derby, Irish Derby and King George VI and Queen Elizabeth Diamond Stakes.

SIGNORINETTA (1905)
• Chaleureux • Signorina (St Simon)

In the 1880s, Cavaliere Edoardo Ginistrelli came to Newmarket from Italy, bought Oaks Lodge and bred and trained racehorses.

Ginistrelli was regarded as a figure of fun. His reputation was not enhanced when he noticed that his mare Signorina and a cheap stallion called Chaleureux seemed attracted to each other or, as Ginistrelli put it, 'they are in love'. Arranging a love mating resulted in a filly called Signorinetta.

In 1908, dismissing the Form Book in favour of wildly optimistic hope, Ginistrelli despatched Signorinetta to Epsom for the Derby, where she faced 17 colts, all better fancied than her. In her previous race, two weeks earlier, Signorinetta had been unplaced.

Starting at an appropriate 100-1, Signorinetta not only won the Derby comfortably but two days later also won the Oaks. Extraordinary.

> Don't laugh at me. I am going to win the Derby with my pet.
> *Edoardo Ginistrelli to bystanders in Newmarket*

Top-hole names

Entire (1984)
* Relkino • Tactless (Romulus)
Entire was a gelding. Bred and initially owned by Lord Fairhaven,
he won a selling race at Redcar in 1987 and a hurdle at Market Rasen
in 1990.

Lowawatha (1988)
* Dancing Brave • Shorthouse (Habitat)
A word play on Hiawatha, a Native American leader whose name
was made famous by Henry Longfellow's popular poem, *The Song
of Hiawatha* (1855).
Bred and initially owned by Louis Freedman's Cliveden Stud,
Lowawatha won six times on the Flat and once over fences between
1991 and 1997.

Service (2000)
* College Chapel • Centre Court (Second Set)
Won once from 16 starts – a selling race at Yarmouth in 2002
when trained by William Haggas and owned by Tony Doyle and
Lester Piggott.

ULYSSES (2013)
* Galileo • Light Shift (Kingmambo)

The winner of the 2017 Coral-Eclipse Stakes and Juddmonte
International could have been named after many Ulysses: Ulysses
S. Grant, President of the United States; the town of Ulysses; the
legendary figure of Odysseus, in Latin form; the chapter in *The
Wind in the Willows* titled 'The Return of Ulysses', or the novel
by James Joyce.

The colt was probably named after Odysseus, but Odysseus
was incredibly slow – it took him ten years to get home from the

Trojan War – while Ulysses the horse was quick. It's more fun to believe that he was named after Joyce's controversial novel, which covers a single day in the life of Leopold Bloom in 1904.

Ulysses was first published in France in 1922, and was banned in the UK until 1936 and in the USA until 1944, on grounds of obscenity. That did wonders for sales when it became available, although a lot of readers probably failed to follow its stream of consciousness to the end. If you think *Ulysses* is difficult, try Joyce's *Finnegans Wake*. I bet you can't get through that; very few have.

> He has a hell of a pedigree, he has looks, he has quality and he's some athlete. He's hard to fault.
> *Sir Michael Stoute after Ulysses's victory in the Juddmonte International*

Races won: five in 2016 and 2017, notably the Group 1 Coral-Eclipse Stakes and Group 1 Juddmonte International Stakes.

LEOPOLD BLOOM (1986)
● Le Moss ● Barhopper (Avocat)

Not a champion, but he did win a National Hunt Flat race at Fairyhouse in 1991.

> Good puzzle would be cross Dublin without passing a pub.
> *Leopold Bloom in* Ulysses

ULYSSES (2014 – THE GERMAN ONE)
● Sinndar ● Ungarin (Goofalik)

Several other Ulysses have raced in Britain and elsewhere, none of them champions. The latest is a German-bred Ulysses who finished runner-up twice on the Flat in England in 2017 and once over hurdles in 2018. So there's still hope.

ODYSSEUS

Odysseuses have been bred in Brazil and Japan, Australia and
the USA, Ireland and Great Britain. None have been champions
although the USA edition, *Odysseus* (2007) *Malibu Moon –
Persimmon Hill (Conquistador Cielo),* won three times from just
five tries, including the 2010 Grade 3 Tampa Bay Derby.

   More interesting is the legend that Odysseus was turned
into a horse, in one version by Minerva (alias Athene), in another
by a sorceress called Hals.

   When Odysseus came to Hals she reportedly turned him
   into a horse by means of her magical drugs.
   Quoted in NJ Allen, 'Why Did Odysseus Become A Horse?'
   Journal of the Anthropological Society of Oxford *(1995)*

2. DISAPPOINTMENTS AND DELINQUENTS

AMRULLAH (1980)
● High Top ● Ravenshead (Charlottown)

Amrullah is a boy's name meaning a gift from Allah. Trainer John Bridger's miscreant was certainly a boy but hardly a heavenly gift.

By the time he retired, in 1992, Amrullah had run 74 times. He had run but he hadn't tried very hard; well, barely at all, really. If he'd tried he would have won because he had ability but preferred not to use it.

Bridger and Terry Thorn, Amrullah's owner, were incredibly patient and did their best to see the good in Amrullah, rather like prison officers looking for redeeming qualities in a serial killer. Springing to Amrullah's defence, Thorn once remarked, 'He doesn't object to everything. He likes biting and kicking. I was once offered £40,000 for him but I thought that if someone was prepared to pay that much for him he must be worth having, so I kept him. I suppose it was a mistake.'

> Don't worry, it was a lovely clean break.
> *John Bridger to Terry Thorn after Amrullah had broken his wife Gillian's arm.*

Races won: None.

Fag-end names

Give Mea Fag (1984)
• Pollerton • Twelve Steps (Tumble Wind)
Only made one abortive appearance. Probably too ashamed
to make another.

Fag End (1993)
• Treasure Kay • Gauloise Bleue (Lyphard's Wish)
Dam's name a mitigating factor; even so... Won twice in 1995.

BROXADELLA (1980)
• Broxted • Addie (Klairon)

It would be fair to say that Broxadella was not enamoured with racing. In 1982, as a two-year-old, she hinted at her intentions by finishing tailed off last at Wolverhampton. The following year, after reappearing at the same course, the Form Book noted that she 'swerved badly left start, took no part'.

At Ayr, Broxadella 'swerved badly left start' again and was 'always behind'. Her season ended at Beverley with a 'swerved left and unseated rider start, took no part'. Amazingly, Broxadella had started, or not started, as the second favourite.

In 1984 the miscreant was 'unruly' and 'refused to race' at Warwick, before crowning her Flat career at Pontefract. Broxadella shot out of stall 13, whipped round and shot back into stall 11. After that she 'whipped round start' and 'took no part'.

Neither the Jockey Club nor Timeform were impressed. The former banned her from the Flat, while the latter awarded Broxadella their dreaded double squiggle and stated that she 'has gone completely the wrong way temperamentally and must be left severely alone'.

Trainer Arthur Jones agreed and left Broxadella's jumping career to Tony Brisbourne. On her hurdling debut at Bangor in 1987 it took three helpers to get jockey Mark Brisbourne on board, after which Broxadella tried to lie down.

Eventually, they set off in last place. By the second hurdle they were 20 lengths clear, after which Broxadella applied the brakes and finished last. The Brisbournes gave the nightmare one more chance, which Broxadella declined. They then passed her on to Peter Davis.

Invited to take part in a novices' chase at Southwell in 1989, Broxadella refused to race. She rounded off her career by bolting in a hurdle at Nottingham before being tailed off and pulled up.

Races won: you're joking.

A jolly bad name

Semolina (1887)
• St Simon • Mowerina (Scottish Chief)

The 6th Duke of Portland must have gone to a school where they didn't serve semolina pudding for lunch, or he wouldn't have been able to bear being reminded of it. Dreadful stuff, made only slightly more palatable by a dollop of jam in the middle.

Luckily for Portland, his Semolina was a prolific winner as a two-year-old and went on to win the 1890 1,000 Guineas.

GO WEST YOUNG MAN (2008)
• Westerner • Last Of Her Line (Silver Patriarch)

On 2 May 2016, at Kempton, Go West Young Man did an extraordinary thing. After being reluctant to let Jake Greenall get on board (that wasn't the extraordinary thing), he won a handicap hurdle on the bit. It was the eight-year-old's 18th race. Sixteen races and two years later, it was still Go West Young Man's only victory. Then, amazingly, the rascal finally won again, at 20-1.

Go West Young Man had finished second nine times and third four times, because he has ability but lacks the desire to use it.

Trainer Henry Daly and owner-breeder Tim Nixon steadfastly kept hoping and probably praying.

Early signs of delinquency reached fruition at Uttoxeter in 2014 when Go West Young Man ran out. Two races later, at Exeter, he put up a spectacular display, leading before the final hurdle, drawing clear on the run in then suddenly executing a 90-degree turn that took him from the far to the near rail and from first to sixth place.

Sent off favourite for a maiden hurdle at Bangor in 2016, Go West Young Man was 'behind when hung right and went off course after last, came to standstill'. As he gained experience, Go West Young Man showed himself to be a cut above the ordinary offender. After raising hopes by winning at Kempton, Go West Young Man was sent to Aintree for the appropriately named Will She/Won't She Handicap Hurdle. The miscreant 'was reluctant to go to the start and then, after pulling his way to the front, applied the brakes, passing the entrance to the paddock with a circuit to go and deposited his jockey on the ground'. The jockey was Tom O'Brien, regular partner Jake Greenall possibly having told Daly that he'd love to ride the horse again but had to wash his hair.

Six months later, at Bangor, journalist Tony McFadden reported, 'The enigmatic Go West Young Man put on such an energetic display of dancing in the parade ring that his owner may be well advised to enter him in the next series of Britain's Got Talent.'

At Huntingdon in November 2017, having eventually condescended to start, Go West Young Man veered left towards the stables instead of right around the bend, crashed into the rails and unseated Mr Hugh Nugent.

Daly and Nixon finally gave up the unequal battle. In May 2018 Go West Young Man was sold for an undeserved £5,000 to Laura Morgan. Reappearing in cheekpieces at Market Rasen, Go West Young Man tried not to start and finished well beaten. Then, at Perth in July, armed with a visor and Miss Tabitha Worsley, Go West Young Man led most of the way to win over £13,000. Well done. Only for a while. Six days later, at Market Rasen, the new hero led his rivals a merry dance, then ducked out at the sixth fence.

Races won: two.

Two more jolly bad names

The Slug (2004)
• Tamayaz • Snow Huntress (Shirley Heights)

What a name to give a racehorse. Granted, he was pretty slow, failing to win in ten races under Rules in Ireland, but winning four point-to-points in England in 2010 and 2011.

The Snail (2003)
• Namaqualand • Moonshine Malt (Superlative)

Admirably, refused to be defined by his insulting name and won seven jumps races between 2008 and 2010, followed by four point-to-point successes in 2012 and 2013.

GREEN GREEN DESERT (1991)
• Green Desert • Green Leaf (Alydar)

Life is full of disappointments and for many race fans Green Green Desert was one of them. Expectations were high (usually a mistake in racing) after Michael Stoute's two-year-old 'looked a thumping good colt in the making' when quickening in 'spectacular' fashion to win on his debut at Newmarket. The highly respected Timeform *Racehorses of 1993* deemed it 'one of the most striking sights we saw all season', and envisaged that Green Green Desert could develop into 'a live contender for the 2,000 Guineas'.

Unfortunately, 13 races, two seasons and one gelding operation later, Green Green Desert had failed to win again, although he had started favourite five times, finished second five times and third three times. Sold for 36,000 guineas at the end of 1995 and sent to Lady Herries, Green Green Desert continued in the same vein, finishing runner-up twice and third twice.

Disillusionment reached *Racehorses of 1996*, which noted that the five-year-old, although consistent, was 'irresolute and one to treat with caution'.

Yet if Green Green Desert had been able to speak (he couldn't), he could have mounted a strong defence. An unlikely jumper, Green Green Desert went on to win twice over hurdles and seven times over fences for trainers Oliver Sherwood and Paul Nicholls. He was best when able to win without too much effort being required but few horses boast a record of ten wins, 13 second places and nine third places from 55 appearances, earning over £135,000.

Take Green Green Desert out of this section immediately.

Races won: ten, including £13,600 Mitsubishi Shogun Trophy Chase at Ayr in 1999.

A name deserving a black mark

Salmonella (1979)
• Big Kohinoor • Kaysirmo (Dear Sir)
Calling a horse after bacteria that causes food poisoning makes Salmonella a leading candidate for the worst name in modern times. Miraculously, racing in the USA, he won nine races between 1981 and 1985, albeit little ones. Salmonella's total earnings were only $27,334.

HARWELL LAD (1989)
• Over The River • Gayles Approach (Strong Gale)

Hero and villain (see also Knockroe and Vodkatini, below). It's a bit harsh branding Harwell Lad a delinquent, considering that he won the Whitbread Gold Cup and five other races, as well as three point-to-points. Harsh, yet fair.

Owned throughout his chequered career by Harry Wellstead, trained by Robert Alner and ridden, in a tremendous test of character and horsemanship, by Mr Rupert Nuttall, Harwell Lad graduated from point-to-pointing in 1995. The six-year-old got off to a cracking start, winning his first four chases – 'made all, easily', 'easily' and 'easily' again.

Yet all was not quite well. At Wincanton, Harwell Lad was 'reluctant to race and ran wide on bend. Soon well behind'. Luckily for enthusiasts laying horses on betting exchanges, Betfair did not arrive until 2000, so they were spared watching Harwell Lad then make 'rapid headway to regain lead three out' and win by 15 lengths.

Unlike Vodkatini, who was sometimes reluctant to start, Harwell Lad was prepared to start but sometimes reluctant to continue.

In 1996 the equine enigma achieved comments such as 'refused to race from tenth' (Chepstow), 'reluctant to race' (Sandown) and 'tried to pull up before 11th' (Ascot). As a result, Harwell Lad was 14-1 when appearing at Towcester, where he was seen 'jumping splendidly in front' on his way to victory.

In 1997, after running creditably at Chepstow, Harwell Lad emerged as the unlikely winner of the prestigious Whitbread Gold Cup. Falling back either exhausted or disenchanted, the temporary hero went into irredeemable decline, registering 'reluctant to race tenth' (Cheltenham), 'reluctant to race' (Ascot), and pulling up twice before exiting the stage at Sandown in 1998 when 'virtually refused to race after tenth'.

If it hadn't been for hunting, this horse would have ended up in meat cans.
Rupert Nuttall after winning the Whitbread Gold Cup.
Nuttall was Master of the Blackmore and Sparkford Vale
Hunt, and ascribed Harwell Lad's (intermittent) success to his
days in the hunting field

Races won: 1997 Whitbread Gold Cup and five other chases.

A likeable name

Letthebighossroll (1988)
* Flying Paster * Moonlight Jig (Jig Time)
One of Mike Pegram's (of whom more if you keep reading),
Letthebighossroll, racing in California, won 18 races and over $1 million
between 1991 and 1997. I just like the name.

KNOCKROE (1968)
* Fortino II * Corbalton (Milesian)

A personal favourite, both a champion and a delinquent, Knockroe perfected the art of exasperating people. He exasperated his owner, Major Victor McCalmont, he exasperated his trainer, Major Peter Nelson, he exasperated his riders, and he drove an assortment of punters, few of them majors, mad.

Knockroe was exasperating at home, where special measures were required to persuade him to set off up the gallops, involving banging on the roof of a car, and exasperating at the racecourse, where he sometimes condescended to take part and win but sometimes didn't.

'He was quite impossible,' said McCalmont. 'People were always telling me how intelligent he was but he wasn't, he was a bloody fool.' Perhaps Knockroe overheard him and took offence.

Knockroe liked to race in splendid isolation and to spend most of each race a disturbing distance behind his rivals. When he felt like it, he'd use his fine turn of foot to steam to victory; when he didn't, he wouldn't. Patience and tolerance were essential. As jockey Eric Eldin explained, 'You couldn't lose your temper, because if he was extra-miserable, you were in trouble. If you moved a muscle, he wouldn't go. You didn't wait with him, he waited with you.'

Despite what might politely be described as 'eccentricities', Knockroe won two Group 2 and three Group 3 races in 1971 and 1972. 1973 didn't go as well. In three successive races, Knockroe

declined to play an active part, with the result that he started
at 20-1 for the Weetabix Wildlife Handicap at Epsom's Derby
meeting. Carrying top weight, Knockroe broke the course record
set by Mahmoud when winning the Derby 37 years previously.

> He had supreme natural ability. Snow Knight [1974
> Derby winner] was a good, genuine horse but Knockroe
> was better. If he had given his all, he would have been
> unbeatable, but the horse had a peculiar temperament.
> *Peter Nelson*

Races won: 1971 Group 3 Cumberland Lodge Stakes; 1972 Group 2
Jockey Club Stakes and Yorkshire Cup, Group 3 Cumberland Lodge
Stakes and St Simon Stakes.

LEVARAMOSS (1973)
• Levmoss • Tandara (Tanerko)

It takes a high-class delinquent to be banned from the
racecourse. Step forward (something he often wasn't prepared
to do) Levaramoss.

Levaramoss failed to win in four runs on the Flat but
immediately showed a talent for hurdling, winning three of his
first four races in 1976/77 for trainer Staff Ingham and conditional
jockey Anton Gonsalves.

After Ingham's death in 1977 his son Tony took over the
responsibility for Levaramoss, who was already attracting comments
such as 'ridden all the way' and, on his final outing of the season
when odds-on favourite at Fontwell, 'virtually refused to start'.

Perhaps mollified by a break, Levaramoss started the 1977/78
season by winning the Free Handicap Hurdle at Chepstow,
making all under former champion jump jockey Bob Davies.
Unfortunately, Levaramoss was no respecter of jockeys. Three
weeks later, when odds-on favourite at Newbury, Levaramoss
refused to race.

He quickly made up for it by winning the Lansdown Hurdle at Cheltenham. Performing like a yo-yo, Levaramoss was soon reluctant to race at Cheltenham, won at Fontwell, refused to race at Windsor and Kempton and, out of his depth in the 1978 Champion Hurdle, started slowly and was always tailed off. By then with trainer Mick Bolton, Levaramoss rounded the season off by virtually refusing to race at Ascot.

His next appearance – unplaced – was in 1979 and after another year off, Levaramoss was switched to fences. After finishing third at Wincanton, the enigma was then reluctant to race, refused at the first fence at Cheltenham, was tailed off and pulled up over hurdles at Folkestone and, back over fences, refused at the first fence at Lingfield.

The Jockey Club thought that was enough, and in 1981 Levaramoss and racing under Rules were compulsorily divorced.

Races won: six, because Levaramoss was a good hurdler when he felt like it.

No, I don't think so

Spineless Jellyfish (1996)
• Skywalker • Silky Sand Sammy (Desert Wine)
Some jellyfish! The colt won ten times for trainer Jenine Sahadi in California between 1998 and 2004, earning almost $900,000.

MAD MOOSE (2004)
• Presenting • Sheshollystar (Fourstars Allstar)

'He was just cleverer than us,' trainer Nigel Twiston-Davies concluded after years of trying to find the key to the appropriately named Mad Moose. Twiston-Davies tried hard because when Mad Moose condescended to race he was good at it. Bought for €11,000 in 2008, Mad Moose enjoyed a golden spell between August 2010 and September 2011, winning five jumps races. The following spring he won again, was given a summer break and on his return, at Cheltenham, showed his gratitude by refusing to race.

There were some creditable performances along the bumpy way to the 2013 Cheltenham Festival, notably when runner-up to Sprinter Sacre in the Victor Chandler Chase, but at Cheltenham Mad Moose refused to race again. He wasn't impressed by Aintree, either, refusing to race in the Melling Chase.

In an act of genius or desperation, Twiston-Davies ran Mad Moose, by then a nine-year-old, in a Flat race at Doncaster. Experiencing starting stalls for the first time, Mad Moose won at 28-1. He was immediately promoted to the Group 3 Ormonde Stakes at Chester, earning £16,125 by finishing second to the high-class Mount Athos.

Unfortunately, Mad Moose could not be fooled a third time and at York in 2013 emerged from the stalls but then stood still.

On to Royal Ascot and the Queen Alexandra Stakes. 'Reluctant to race,' recorded the Form Book, 'and started very slowly. Took little interest.' Returned to fences, Mad Moose was 'reluctant to race and lost all chance with very slow start'.

Mad Moose happily accepted defeat but his trainer was less willing to give up. To make Mad Moose's position clear, in the 2013 Tingle Creek Chase at Sandown, he 'set off on terms but refused to race properly and pulled himself up before the first'.

In January 2014 the British Horseracing Authority announced that 'with immediate effect no further entries would be accepted for Mad Moose'.

All was not quite lost; that happened in December 2014 when, after obtaining a reprieve from the BHA, Mad Moose was allowed one more try, in a hurdle race at Cheltenham. By then he had his own Twitter account and followers campaigning to 'Let the Moose loose.' The Moose refused to race.

It was him all over. He was walking around at the start
fine and walked in with the rest of them but the minute
the tapes went up he just stopped.
*Jockey Sam Twiston-Davies after a chase at Cheltenham
in October 2012*

Races won: three hurdles, three chases and a Flat race. Mad Moose
also finished second six times and third six times, winning over
£100,000 in prize money. Not bad for a delinquent.

A good name

Cut The Talk (1971)
• The Axe II • Hot Gossip (Correspondent)
A peripatetic performer who ran at nine different tracks in the US
between 1974 and 1982, latterly mainly at Penn National, and won
an impressive 25 times. It's a pity they weren't better races or he'd
have earned more than $137,461.

MARINSKY (1974)
• Northern Dancer • Thong (Nantallah)

While Ubedizzy (see below, if you can be bothered) bit people,
Marinsky bit horses. It was unfortunate as Marinsky had cost
$225,000 (equal to £1.1 million today) at the 1975 Keeneland
Yearling Sales and had the ability to be worth several times that.
   Trained by Vincent O'Brien and racing in the colours of
Coolmore syndicate member Alan Clore, Marinsky saw observers
wax lyrical after his imperious debut at the Curragh in 1976.
Starting at 7-2 on, the beautifully bred half-brother to Thatch
and King Pellinore beat 15 other newcomers by three lengths.
   Asked to do nothing more until 1977, Marinsky started the
season in contempt of his odds of 7-1 on when beaten at the
Curragh by the not very good Sun Rod, whose sole victory

it was in 15 runs that year. Cherished ante-post vouchers for the 2,000 Guineas plummeted in value.

In the Diomed Stakes at Epsom, Marinsky first attacked Relkino and then put his expensive head in the air and declined to make the effort Lester Piggott wanted him to.

Muzzled and blinkered for his next appearance, in the St James's Palace Stakes at Royal Ascot, Marinsky was deemed by the Form Book to have been 'not resolute' when beaten a head by Don.

Switched to six furlongs for the July Cup, Marinsky, again muzzled and blinkered, won comfortably. Unfortunately, he also hung and bumped the runner-up, Gentilhombre. Today he would almost certainly have kept the race but the stewards reversed the placings and subsequently asked O'Brien for an undertaking not to run Marinsky in England again. A month later the reluctant hero died of a twisted gut. Maybe he'd always had stomach ache. He was certainly a pain.

Races won: 1976, a maiden race for two-year-olds at the Curragh.

More black marks

Machine (1968)
• Tutankhamen • Princess Lee (Princely Gift)

Racehorses are sometimes referred to as 'machines' with 'big engines' but they shouldn't be; that's cars. Machine won a Flat race at Galway in 1972 and another at Chepstow in 1974 but spent most of the rest of his life failing to win over jumps. Maybe his engine wasn't big enough.

Industrialist (1970)
• Charlottown • Soie (Shantung)

An awful name for a horse. No wonder he was still a maiden after six tries, then retired.

RICKS NATURAL STAR (1989)
• Natural Native • Malaysian Star (Crimson Star)

It wasn't the horse that was the delinquent, although he was
a disappointment to his eccentric owner and trainer Dr William
Livingston. Looking back, it was a sad story.

Livingston, a veterinarian who believed he'd discovered
a cure for navicular disease, drove Ricks Natural Star over 1,700 miles
from New Mexico to Woodbine racetrack in Toronto to take on some
of the best horses in the world in the 1996 Breeders' Cup Turf.

The seven-year-old hadn't raced for 15 months, before which he'd
run three times in a month at Ruidoso Downs in New Mexico,
finishing last each time. None of the races were worth more than
$1,320 to the winner and Ricks Natural Star could be claimed
for $3,500. Livingston had bought Ricks Natural Star in 1996
for $3,000. He had faith in his horse and faith in his vaccines
and saw the Breeders' Cup as an opportunity to promote them.
He borrowed $40,000 to cover the entry fees and set off.

To the Breeders' Cup authorities' horror, when only 13 other
horses were entered for the race, Ricks Natural Star was eligible
for the final slot. Livingston had no training experience but the
New Mexico Racing Commission had issued him with a licence,
although not with a saddle or bridle. Jockey Lisa McFarland
offered to supply both and to exercise the horse.

Ricks Natural Star had never raced on grass, nor beyond a mile.
Inevitably, he finished tailed off behind Pilsudski but he did finish,
despite not being officially credited with 14th place.

On 15 November, Ricks Natural Star ran against quarter
horses at Los Alamitos, in California. The track had agreed to pay
Livingston $5,000 appearance money and $40,000 if the horse
won. He finished sixth of seven.

Two months later the unlikely celebrity appeared at Turf
Paradise, in Arizona. After finishing eighth of ten, Ricks Natural
Star was claimed by Larry Weber for $7,500. Weber bought him
for the horse's sake and promptly retired Ricks Natural Star to

Jeff Thornbury's Sunnyside Farm in Kentucky. He lived there
contentedly until dying at the ripe old age of 29 in 2017.

We're going to win it. Put $300 on him and get yourself
a new car.
*Dr William Livingston to the author, outside the barn
at Woodbine before the Breeders' Cup*

Races won: two, both in New Mexico in 1993.

UBEDIZZY (1973)
• Carnival Dancer • Ermyn Lass (Ennis)

He was called Ubedizzy but often a lot of other names too, rude
and well deserved. Ubedizzy is long gone but his teethmarks live
on, as Andy Crook can testify.

Crook, now training in Yorkshire, looked after Ubedizzy at
Steve Nesbitt's Middleham yard. There wasn't a long queue for the
job, even though Ubedizzy became a high-class sprinter, winning
eight times in Britain and finishing fourth in the 1977 William
Hill Sprint Championship (now the Nunthorpe Stakes) at York
and second in the 1978 Abernant Stakes at Newmarket.

That was Ubedizzy's last race in Britain, as his post-race
performance was one bite too many for the Jockey Club. In the
unsaddling enclosure, Ubedizzy knocked over his groom, pinned
him to the ground and despite wearing a muzzle, tried to bite him.
He had already bitten Crook, leaving him with one finger shorter
than it should be. At least Crook won four races on Ubedizzy, who
ended up in Sweden with trainer Claes von Arnold, for whom he
won a Listed sprint in 1979.

If I was offered £1,000 a week to do him now, I wouldn't
do it. The times I used to come out of his box with a leg
missing off my trousers or my shirt torn to bits ...
Andy Crook

Races won: 1976 William Hill Trophy Handicap; 1977 Chesterfield Handicap; 1979 Lanwades Stud Jagersro Sprint; six other races.

VODKATINI (1979)
* Dubassoff * Olympic Visualise (Northfields)

As herd animals, thoroughbreds can be expected to avoid being left behind for fear of being eaten by lions. Vodkatini, a mixture of vodka and dry vermouth with an olive and twist of lemon, wasn't convinced. Perhaps he had worked out that there weren't any lions roaming Sandown Park and that racing was hard work and involved running around in circles and possibly falling over.

To begin with, he took the opposite approach and led the field, fast. On his first run over hurdles, at Newbury in 1982, Vodkatini led until approaching the second last, where he ran out. Five days later, at Plumpton, he led until the winning post, where he was 15 lengths clear.

For trainer Peter Haynes it was a mixture of good and bad but after Vodkatini joined Josh Gifford in 1987 the good was temporarily in the ascendant, with Vodkatini winning five of the next season's eight chases. The victories weren't straightforward. Vodkatini bolted on the way to the start before winning at Fontwell at the end of 1987. Two months later, at Kempton, he whipped round at the start and lost 20 lengths before going on to win. His career climaxed at the 1988 Cheltenham Festival, when Vodkatini won the Grand Annual Chase.

He won another three times in 1988/89, but those successes were overshadowed by the delinquent's behaviour in the Tingle Creek Chase at Sandown and Captain Morgan Chase at Aintree. Favourite for both, Vodkatini declined to start, much to the annoyance of everyone apart from his rivals.

Vodkatini raced on, sometimes, until 1992, when he was 13, but he didn't win again. He was hardly a failure, winning 13 times, finishing runner-up seven times and occupying high rank among two-mile chasers. It was just that he could have done even better if he'd wanted to.

He was absolutely flying at home and I thought there was no way they could beat us. Everything was perfect. He lined up lovely, then the tapes went up and he just refused point-blank to move.

Jockey Richard Rowe on Vodkatini at the start of the 1988 Tingle Creek Chase

Races won: 13 including the 1988 Grand Annual Challenge Cup at Cheltenham.

Gold star names

Polygamy (1971)

• Reform • Seventh Bride (Royal Record)

The first foal of Seventh Bride, bred and owned by Louis Freedman's Cliveden Stud. Polygamy won the 1974 Oaks and four other races.

One Over Parr (1972)

• Reform • Seventh Bride (Royal Record)

Seventh Bride's second foal, One Over Parr had one of the cleverest names ever bestowed on a racehorse. Henry VIII's sixth and final wife was Catherine Parr. One Over Parr won the Cheshire Oaks and Lancashire Oaks in 1975 and two other races.

Bedfellow (1973)

• Crepello • Seventh Bride (Royal Record)

Seventh Bride's third foal failed to match her half-sisters' achievements but won two races in 1975 and 1976.

3. HORSES WITH NO NAMES AND NAMES WITH TWO HORSES

It's obvious that in a horse race the horses need to have names, different names. Yet in 1866 a race was arranged between a three-year-old colt called Robin Hood, owned by Lord Portsmouth, and another three-year-old colt also called Robin Hood, owned by Baron Mayer de Rothschild. It was a condition of the race that the loser must 'drop the Hood'. Lord Portsmouth's Robin Hood was the victor and Baron Rothschild's Robin Hood subsequently raced as Robin.

At that time, plenty of racehorses shared the same name. In 1859 there were 44 cases of horses with the same name, including three four-year-olds all named Sunbeam. Horses sometimes started the season under one name and ended it under another. William Hill would have gone mad.

Until 1913 it was permissible to run any horse without a name, provided the dam's name and the horse's sex were indicated. Until 1946 two-year-olds could still run nameless.

Today every horse must have a name and a microchip in its neck for identification. It's not foolproof. In July 2017 the previously unraced Mandarin Princess sprang a surprise by winning a race for two-year-olds at Yarmouth, at 50-1. It was less of a surprise when it emerged that the horse was actually a three-year-old stablemate, Millie's Kiss. A three-year-old would have a big advantage over two-year-olds.

It was the result of a muddle rather than skulduggery but it triggered a change in procedures. As well as horses being scanned for microchip identification on arrival at racecourse stables, they were to be scanned again before each race.

Even that wasn't foolproof. At Southwell in January 2018, trainer Ivan Furtado's African Trader and Scribner Creek ran in the wrong races. The mistake was discovered the next day and the horses were disqualified. More procedural changes followed.

HE-HAS-A-NAME, GIVE-HIM-A-NAME
AND HE-ISN'T-WORTH-A-NAME

According to 'Thormanby' (William Willmott Dixon), writing in his *Famous Racing Men* (1882), the 5th Earl of Glasgow (1792–1869) 'always said that a horse should not be named till he had earned a name by winning a race and, as his horses rarely, considering their number, achieved that distinction, they were for the most part shot unnamed'.

'Thormanby' used the word 'shot' advisedly, as the Earl of Glasgow had a habit of ordering trainers to shoot horses on the gallops if they failed to run fast enough. Since the obstinate Earl persisted in breeding horses with unpromising pedigrees, a lot were shot – reputedly six in a single morning on one occasion.

'No man probably in the history of the Turf,' wrote 'Thormanby', 'ever brought out so many bad horses.' The exception was General Peel, who won the 2,000 Guineas in 1864 and was runner-up in both the Derby and St Leger.

To make matters worse, the Earl of Glasgow liked to run and back his horses in matches, which usually resulted in costly defeats. Fortunately, he had an annual income of between £60,000 (about £5 million today) and £150,000 (about £12 million).

Lacking patience and with a strong sense of aristocratic superiority, Lord Glasgow regularly changed both trainers and waiters. Unhappy with a waiter at the Black Swan Inn in York, he threw him out of the window and told a surviving member of staff to 'put him on the bill'. The waiter broke an arm and £5 was added to his Lordship's bill. The Black Swan Inn is still there and it would be interesting to see if the window has been repaired, as well as the waiter.

Lord Derby and other Jockey Club friends tried, usually unsuccessfully, to persuade the Earl of Glasgow to name his horses. On one occasion he succumbed as far as to name three horses:

HE-HAS-A-NAME (1839)
• Retainer • St Patrick mare

GIVE-HIM-A-NAME (1838)
• Muley Moloch • Actaeon mare

AND **HE-ISN'T-WORTH-A-NAME**

He-isn't-worth-a-name's future was clearly precarious, to the extent that he may never have reached a racecourse.

Glasgow's friend Colonel Peel had similar inclinations. At Newmarket in 1843, Peel's I-am-not-aware beat Give-him-a-name in a match. Not satisfied with having been beaten once, Lord Glasgow arranged a repeat match later the same day, with the same outcome. The *Sporting Magazine* reported that Give-him-a-name 'ran gamely but slowly'.

MYHORSEWITHNONAME (2014)
• Lilbourne Lad • Colleville (Pharly)

In 2016, Michael Baldry bought an unraced and unnamed two-year-old for £1,000 and sent it to trainer Natalie Lloyd-Beavis at East Garston, near Lambourn.

Baldry, a cousin of the late, great 'Long John' Baldry, had staff working with horses at his own home in Sussex and they'd ask, 'How's the horse with no name?' So, before the horse made its racing debut that September, Baldry named it Myhorsewithnoname.

The Earl of Glasgow would have approved although, as Myhorsewithnoname has finished last in all four runs to date, beaten a total of almost 200 lengths, the Earl might have reached for his shotgun.

So let the heartaches begin
I can't help it, I can't win.
'Long John' Baldry, 'Let the Heartaches Begin', 1967

Races won: none so far, and victory doesn't seem likely.

REFUSED A NAME (2007)
• Montjeu • Dixielake (Lake Coniston)

Dr Breandan Long, an orthopaedic surgeon, was the proud owner
of an unnamed gelding with trainer John Joseph 'Shark' Hanlon,
in County Carlow. All the gelding lacked was a name.

'We put in about ten names,' Hanlon recalls, 'and all of them
were turned back. So in the end we put up Refused A Name and
that was accepted.'

Were the rejected names rude? On that, Hanlon was coy.

Races won: three chases in Ireland in 2013 and 2014.

NAMELESS (1993)
• Doc Marten • Opuntia (Rousillon)

Nameless wasn't always Nameless. The filly was first registered as
Wear The Fox Hat and it was only when trainer David Cosgrove
entered her for a race that the name was queried.

Cosgrove received a phone call from the Jockey Club to say
that Wear The Fox Hat could not run under that name, followed
by a visit from a Weatherbys' representative. He took the horse's
passport away and Cosgrove and the owner, Julian Wilson (not
the BBC television presenter), renamed her Nameless.

Races won: two, both at Wolverhampton, in 1995.

That wasn't the end of Wear The Fox Hat. Between 2013 and 2015
a filly owned and bred by the Jedburgh Stud in Normandy raced

22 times under that name in France for trainer Stuart Cargeeg. In 2014, as a three-year-old, she won a small race at Marseille.

No-name names

No Name Needed (2010)
• Medaglia d'Oro • Take Me Home (Housebuster)
Ran just three times, in the US, winning on her debut at Hollywood Park in 2012.

What's His Name (2010)
• Rocky Bar • Dancing Buckaroo (Thorn Dance)
Bred in Idaho, where they hardly have racing. In 2013 What's His Name won twice at Les Bois Park, the State's biggest racetrack. Les Bois Park closed in 2015.

YOUCANTCALLHERTHAT (2011)
• Brian Boru • Fruitful Venture (Fruits Of Love)

Four of the friends belonging to the Lostwelton Syndicate – Alan Burke, Darren and Iarlaith Collins and Diarmaid Gavin – were sitting at a kitchen table discussing what to call their unnamed mare. She didn't like water but when someone suggested calling her Aquaphobia, a voice from the kitchen sink, belonging to Peggy Murphy, immediately said, 'You can't call her that!' So they called her Youcantcallherthat.

It worked out wonderfully well because having considered selling her, the hyper-enthusiastic syndicate were able to watch her win five chases in 2017 and 2018. They included a Grade 2 chase at Limerick and a Grade 3 chase at Fairyhouse.

4. WEATHERBYS –
THE NEXUS OF NAMES

In 1770, James Weatherby was appointed Secretary to the Jockey Club and Keeper of the Match Book. The latter's role was not to look after the matches, although that's important if you're working with flammable materials rather than horses, but to deal with races and their stake and prize money. Subsequently, Weatherbys became the Jockey Club's administrative branch and now supplies administrative services to the British Horseracing Authority.

Mike Butts is Head of Racing and Alison Wade Supervisor of the Names Team, who work closely with their counterparts in Ireland. There are about 250,000 registered names with about 16,000 registered each year in Great Britain and Ireland. It means that Butts, who has been with Weatherbys for over 20 years, and Wade, who has been there for over 30 years, will have seen more rude names than most people.

Technology has changed procedures. Nowadays registering names is a very slick and quick process, with a 24-hour turnaround.

People can check online to see if a name is available and if it appears to be, can reserve it. There are roughly 3,000 names on a domestic list of 'protected names' and similarly on a much shorter international list. The names of 'well-known horses' cannot be duplicated while those of 'public persons' are banned. Any person must be dead for 50 years before his or her name can be used without their permission. If they've been dead for more than 50 years it is still difficult to get their permission but you can just go ahead and assume it's okay with them.

Then there are 'names which are suggestive or have a vulgar, obscene or insulting meaning; names considered in poor taste or names that may be offensive to religious, political or ethnic groups or, in the opinion of the BHA, may cause offence.'

This represents a tempting challenge and there has long been a battle between owners trying to register a risqué or crude name and the Weatherbys team trying to foil them. As the section titled Sexcetera (you've probably already read it) reveals, some dubious names have sneaked through.

'We use an urban dictionary now,' says Wade. 'It's the same owners and names that keep appearing. We also have a list of non-desirable names that have been turned down in the past by the BHA.'

Weatherbys never had to cope with Big Tits (see Sexcetera section), who ran in France in 2003 and 2004. The shared view of Butts and Wade is, 'If Big Tits had come from France to race here, the BHA could have asked for the name to be changed or refused permission for it to run.'

And if the name-checkers were choosing a name themselves? Mike Butts says, 'I'd have liked there to have been a horse by Paris House out of Ladycake and it been called Chateau Gateau.' There was a Paris House and a Ladycake but, sadly, no Chateau Gateau.

5. COLLECTIONS

Colonel Bradley's Bs

He wasn't a real Colonel, although Edward Riley Bradley (1859–1946) was honoured with the title by the Governor of Kentucky for his contribution to horseracing. The Colonel's contribution owed a lot to his and brother Jack's Beach Club in Palm Beach, Florida. Opened in 1898, it offered dining but also gambling.

In the same year, Bradley won his first horse race with Friar John at the Harlem racetrack in Illinois. In 1903, having won $9,000 (equivalent to $253,000 or more today) in a plunge on a horse called Brigade, Bradley bought Bad News for $7,500.

BAD NEWS (1900)
* Flying Dutchman * Black Sleeves (Sir Dixon)

Bad News had recently finished fourth in the Kentucky Derby. When Bradley asked its owners, Messrs Woodward and Buckner, why they had called the colt Bad News, he was told it was because they had 'heard that bad news travels fast'. They were right. Bad News won 47 races for Bradley during the next eight years and finished with a career total of 54 wins from 185 races.

In 1906, Bradley bought a stud in Lexington and named it the Idle Hour Stock Farm. In the next 40 years, thanks greatly to the success of the broodmare La Troienne, bought at Newmarket in 1930, the stud made a huge impact.

With Brigade and Bad News close to his heart, Bradley decided to give all his horses names beginning with the letter B. There were a great many of them, including some very good ones.

Bradley not only won the Kentucky Derby four times, with Behave Yourself (1921), Bubbling Over (1926), Burgoo King (1932) and Brokers Tip (1933), but on two occasions (1921 and 1926) had the runner-up as well (Black Servant and Bagenbaggage). Bradley's Bs won the Preakness Stakes three times and Belmont Stakes twice, with Bimelech winning both in 1940. Several of his horses were named either Horse of the Year or declared Champions in one category or another, including Blue Larkspur (1929), Barn Swallow (1933), Bazaar (1934), Black Helen (1935), Busher (1945) and Bridal Flower (1946).

Hoping, perhaps, to be lucky twice, Bradley named another horse Bad News (1929). The colt wasn't nearly as good as his namesake but did win eight times.

> **Senator Huey Long:** 'What is your business?'
> **Colonel Edward R. Bradley:** 'I am a speculator, I breed and race horses and gamble.'
> **Senator Huey Long:** 'Do you confine your gambling to racehorses?'
> **Colonel Edward R. Bradley:** 'I gamble on anything.'
> *United States Senate Committee on Finance hearing,*
> *4 April 1934. Huey 'The Kingfish' Long was the former*
> *Governor of Louisiana, where Bradley once owned the*
> *Fair Grounds racetrack.*

Guy Reed's Cowboys and Indians

Jesus may have turned water into wine but Guy Reed turned chickens into horses.

When he was young, Reed probably liked playing Cowboys and Indians, because a lot of his many horses were given names from the Wild West.

In 1962 Reed and his brother Eric bought Buxted Chickens for £1.9 million (£39 million today) and within five years were able to produce 40 million birds a year, accounting for about a quarter of the UK market. What a revolting thought. It makes you admire vegetarians.

Having sold Buxted, Reed made another fortune with Reed Boardall, a cold storage and transport company.

In 1968 Reed started to breed racehorses. There was Warpath and Dakota, Shotgun and Mohican, Choctaw, Apache, Geronimo and many more. By the time of his death, in 2013, Reed had won over 500 races although it was 2005 before his first Group 1 success, with La Cucaracha.

We will be known forever by the tracks we leave.
Dakota proverb

I was born where there were no enclosures.
Geronimo (1829–1909). The Apache leader never visited a British racecourse enclosure himself but his namesake won six times between 2000 and 2004

Races won: Dakota 1974 King George V Stakes, 1975 Ebor and St Simon Stakes and four other races. La Cucaracha 2005 Nunthorpe Stakes and six other races, including two Group 3 races.

Fine names

Nearly A Fool (1998)
• *Komaite* • *Greenway Lady (Prince Daniel)*
Cleverer than it seems, having been foaled on 31 March. He won nine times between 2000 and 2004.

Oasis Dream (2000)
• *Green Desert* • *Hope (Dancing Brave)*
Dream fulfilled. He won the Group 1 Middle Park Stakes in 2002 and the Group 1 July Cup and Nunthorpe Stakes the following year.

Traffic Jam (2013)
• *Duke of Marmalade* • *Place de L'Etoile (Sadler's Wells)*
A terrific name: the Place de L'Etoile is a notorious road junction in Paris. Trained by Nicolas Clement in France, in 2017 Traffic Jam won the Group 2 Prix du Conseil de Paris at Chantilly.

Lady Beaverbrook and the Gang of Seven

When it comes to names, owners with strings of horses can indulge their passions and eccentricities. Boldboy, Bustino, Mystiko, Niniski, Petoski, Relkino and Terimon were all good horses with two things in common. They were owned by Lady Beaverbrook and had names with seven letters.

Lady Beaverbrook was said to have been influenced by the number of Derby winners with seven letters in their names. When Terimon represented her in the 1989 Derby, four of the previous eight winners of the Classic boasted seven letters – Shergar, Teenoso, Secreto and Kahyasi. You might laugh but Terimon, at 500-1, was only denied by another seven letter contender – Nashwan.

Lady Beaverbrook started life as the splendidly named Marcia Anastasia Christoforides. She saw the beauty in older men and in 1942, aged 32, married Sir James Dunn, aged 67. Despite Dunn's insistence on having his shoelaces ironed, the marriage thrived. In 1954, Salvador Dali ensured Lady Dunn's lasting fame by painting her on horseback in a work entitled *Equestrian Fantasy*.

When Sir James died in 1956 he left half his $65 million (£419 million today) fortune to his widow who, in 1963, aged 52, married Lord Beaverbrook, aged 84. The marriage didn't last – he died a year later.

Neither of her husbands were keen on horseracing but Lady Beaverbrook was. In widowhood she took to the sport with relish and an enormous cheque book. Her racing colours – beaver brown with maple leaf green crossbelts and cap – were a familiar sight on horses trained by Dick Hern and latterly Clive Brittain.

Lady Beaverbrook died in 1994.

You can't run the horse at Salisbury. The lunch there
is terrible.
Lady Beaverbrook to Dick Hern

Races won: Bustino 1974 St Leger, 1975 Coronation Cup; Relkino

1977 Benson and Hedges Gold Cup; Boldboy 1977 Vernons Sprint Cup; Niniski 1979 Irish St Leger and Prix Royal-Oak; Petoski 1985 King George VI and Queen Elizabeth Stakes; Minster Son 1988 St Leger; Mystiko 1991 2,000 Guineas; Terimon 1991 Juddmonte International Stakes.

Names deserving a mention

Bunkered (1966)
* Entanglement • Golf Ball (Persian Gulf)
Trained in Ireland by Kevin Kerr and owned by his brother Bertie, both celebrated sportsmen, Bunkered failed to live up to his name, winning 11 races between 1968 and 1972.

Celibate (1991)
* Shy Groom • Dance Alone (Monteverdi)
Came into his own on the racecourse. Won 14 times between 1994 and 2001, including three Grade 2 chases and the Grade 1 BMW Chase at Punchestown in 1999.

Steven Astaire's Marx Brothers

On 26 August 1991, stockbroker Steven Astaire rode his own horse, Hiram B Birdbath, to victory in an amateur riders' hurdle race at Southwell. It was the highpoint of Astaire's riding career and another step on the road to fame as a racehorse owner.

The names of Astaire's horses belonged not to stars of the sport but to stars of the screen: a resurrection of characters played by Groucho Marx. There was Otis B Driftwood from *A Night at the Opera*, Rufus T Firefly from *Duck Soup* and J Cheever Loophole from *At the Circus*. Not to mention (meaning about to mention) Syrus P Turntable, a variation on the character of almost the same name – Cyrus P Turntable – played by Groucho in an early script for *A Day at the Races*. Then there was Waldorf T Beagle, a crooked lawyer played by Groucho in a 1930s radio programme.

Waldorf T Beagle didn't win a race but most of Astaire's cast of Marx characters did and Hiram B Birdbath, whoever he was (who was he?), won ten times during the 1990s.

Astaire still owns racehorses but seems to have abandoned the Marx Brothers, leaving Mrs Teasdale, from *Duck Soup*, to win at Wolverhampton in July 2017 in the colours of Will Nash.

> **Mrs Claypool:** 'I've been sitting here since seven o'clock.'
> **Otis B Driftwood:** 'Yes, with your back to me. When I invite a woman to dinner I expect her to look at my face. That's the price she has to pay.'
> *A Night at the Opera (1935)*

Races won: Lots, but not big ones.

A nice little name

The Tiddly Tadpole (2005)
• Tipsy Creek • Froglet (Shaamit)
Won three small – as befits a tadpole – hurdle races in 2011/2012.

John Meacock's Persian Delights

Among racing society's rich collection of eccentric owners and trainers, owner-trainer John Meacock occupies a unique place. This is not because, in 1956, while he was working as an estate agent, the case of *John Meacock & Co. v Abrahams* set an important legal precedent in contract law, but because of Meacock's habit of giving his horses Arabic names.

Few other than Meacock knew the meaning of Vakil-ul-Mulk,

Qalibashi, Biyaban Shah, Karkeh Rud, Kouli-Kuh, Khoja Hafiz, Kavar-ul-Mulk, Azad-ul-Mulk, Qebir Kuh, Zardarkuh and a great many others. It was the 1960s, long before the arrival of the Maktoums brought a new generation of unfamiliar racehorse names. Meacock's horses had an exotic flavour and he became a minor cult figure.

Meacock had served in the army in the Middle East and was prone to poetry, often with an oriental air, as in 'The Old Bazaar': exotic but not very good.

> The life of Oriental trade – Pulsates in the bazaars,
> Ancient centre of commerce – Eastern world at large,
> A thousand years – Yet barely changed her face,
> The East does not bustle – Prefers ease to pace.

His horses were much the same, rarely displaying enough pace to win, although Vakil-ul-Mulk, named after a high-ranking Persian official, ran in the 1963 Epsom Derby. He was soon a long way behind but did win several races, mainly after moving to another eccentric trainer, Colonel 'Ricky' Vallance (see entry for Red Candle in Champions section).

Qalibashi won twice in the space of 48 hours at Brighton in 1968. It didn't go unnoticed. In William Trevor's novel *Mrs Eckdorf in O'Neill's Hotel*, published the following year, the hotel owner's son Eugene, a heavy drinker and gambler, reads in a newspaper, 'At Brighton the £35 filly Qalibashi had won at twenty to one.'

That was nothing. In 1966, at Windsor, Karkeh Rud won at 33-1.

> He wore a battered trilby hat, smoked incessantly through
> a cigarette holder, scattering ash indiscriminately, wrote
> unintelligible poetry and was quite the dottiest man that
> I had ever met!
> *Julian Wilson, BBC racing presenter*

Races won: not many but some, especially by Vakil-Ul-Mulk (1960).

He won four times on the Flat in 1965 and 1966, twice for Meacock and twice for Vallance, and six times over hurdles between 1965 and 1968, once for Meacock, three times when trained by Vallance and twice for Les Kennard.

A name without knickers

Knickerless (2003)
• *Fayruz* • *June Lady (Junius)*
Both Knickerless and winless. Finished racing in 2006, possibly to put her knickers on.

Dr Marwan Koukash and the Gabrial Collection

Dr Marwan Koukash's doctoral thesis, 'Analysis Of Change In Surface Form Using Digital Image Processing' (Liverpool Polytechnic, 1987), is less well known than his ownership of racehorses and (2013–18) of the Salford Red Devils Rugby League Club.

Having dipped his toe into horserace ownership in 2007, Koukash dived in and at his equine peak, in 2012, had over 100 horses with 18 trainers. That year they won 101 races.

Koukash got into the habit of naming horses after his son, Gabrial, so that eventually Gabrial's name was borne by over 30 horses. As well as Gabrial, there was Gabrial The Terror, Gabrial The Tyrant, Angel Gabrial, Prince Gabrial, Our Gabrial and many other Gabrials. In 2012, 21 different Gabrials appeared on British racecourses.

As Koukash was particularly fond of Chester, winning the Chester Cup four times, there was sometimes more than one Gabrial running there in the same race. At the start of 2014, the British Horseracing Authority, citing the confusion an excess of Gabrials could cause commentators and the betting public, advised Koukash against creating more.

With his attention focused on the newly acquired Salford Red Devils, Koukash's string of horses shrank. New Gabrials still

occasionally appeared – Gabrial The Devil, Gabrial The Saint
and Gabrials Centurion, all foaled in 2015, were raced in Britain –
but the Gabrial collection was by then a smaller one.

> Finishing second is the first loser. Winning is everything
> in my book; it always will be.
> *Dr Marwan Koukash*

Races won: Gabrial (2009) was the most successful of the Gabrials,
winning eight times, including the 2015 Lincoln Handicap, and
earning over £760,000. Angel Gabrial (2009) won the 2014
Northumberland Plate. Koukash won other big races but not
with Gabrials.

Stan Powell's Stans

On the night of 28 June 1943, the 20-year-old Stanley Kiran Gordon
Powell of 35 Squadron was the navigator on a Halifax bomber
when it was shot down over Liège, in Belgium. Powell parachuted
to relative safety and joined an underground group that tried to
reach Bordeaux. In Paris, he was arrested by the Gestapo and sent
to the Stalag IVB prisoner-of-war camp north of Dresden.

During the next 18 months, Powell made five escape attempts,
the fifth time reaching the Danish border before being captured
and returned to Stalag IVB. He was told that if he tried to escape
again he would be shot. Undeterred, two months later, in March
1945, Powell and another prisoner escaped, reached the Danish
border and waded through a swamp into Denmark and then on
to Sweden and freedom. A year later, Powell was awarded the
Military Cross.

After the war Powell ran an aircraft business at Shoreham
Airport and from the 1960s owned a string of racehorses, mainly
on the Flat with John Sutcliffe and mainly featuring 'Stan' in
their names.

There were lots of them – The Industan and The Andrestan,

The Culstan and The Donstan, The Jeanstan, The Lady Brianstan, The Suestan and many more – so that race fans came to know that horses with names like that belonged to Stan Powell.

Or part-belonged to him. Powell encouraged friends to share the horses and their cost, hence The Brianstan, Le Johnstan and The Adrianstan. When the supply of partners temporarily dried up, Powell named a horse The Solostan. He won eight times.

Not all Powell's horses were Flat horses and not all included 'Stan' in their name. The Chilean-bred Zuko won five times over jumps from Stan Mellor's yard between 1986 and 1990. So there was still a Stan involved.

> 'Stan was a most cheerful person and was always cheering everybody up.'
> *Stan Mellor on Stan Powell after the latter's death in 2000.*

Races won: lots, including a handful of prestigious races.
The Brianstan (1967) won the Prince of Wales's Stakes in 1969 and the Duke of York Stakes in 1971, both at York. In 1972, Le Johnstan (1968) won the Wokingham Stakes at Royal Ascot, and in 1979 The Adrianstan (1975) won the Victoria Cup, also at Ascot.

Oh no, what a name

Plastic Cup (1974)
• Jukebox • Miss Melanie (Hard Ridden)
Despite it being plastic, he drank from the cup of victory five times over hurdles and fences from 1979 to 1981. It's still a rotten name and nowadays he'd be recycled.

Victor Morley-Lawson's Popsies

In horseracing records, Victor Morley-Lawson is best known for having ridden his first winner at the age of 67. The bearded solicitor had been trying for a long time and the golden day finally arrived at Warwick on 16 October 1973, when Ocean King won an amateur riders' Flat race from Moth, ridden by the 22-year-old future champion jumps trainer Nicky Henderson. Henderson will be pleased to be reminded.

The following year, Ocean King, still owned but not ridden by Morley-Lawson, won the Cesarewitch, and in 1980 Popsi's Joy won the same race for him.

Popsi's Joy was the best of the Popsies, a very popular stayer trained, like most of Morley-Lawson's horses, by Mick Haynes and regularly ridden by Lester Piggott. He won 17 times between 1978 and 1985, eight times in 1980, his *annus mirabilis*.

Popsi's Joy's dam was Popsies Pride and her dam was Miss Popsi-Wopsi, who was bred, owned and trained by Morley-Lawson. Miss Popsi-Wopsi won several chases in the late 1950s and early 1960s and at Windsor in January 1961 beat Nicolaus Silver, winner of that year's Grand National. She was ridden in her work by Morley-Lawson's wife Nancy, the daughter of four-times champion jockey Otto Madden, who won the 1898 Derby on Jeddah, at 100-1.

Popsies Pride produced a string of Popsies, including Popsi's Fleece and Popsi's Poppet, who produced Popsi's Legacy, a 25-1 winner at Kempton in 1993. Morley-Lawson was not there to see it, having died in 1988, the year after Popsi's Legacy's birth.

There was to be one more Popsi, also out of Popsi's Poppet, foaled in 1992, bred and trained by Roger Curtis and named, cleverly and cheekily, Popsi's Cloggs. He won a bumper and a chase.

That's quite enough Popsies.

The Cluedo Collection

Cluedo is a murder mystery board game first launched in 1949 with six characters, each suspects in a murder investigation. Ideally Colonel Mustard, Miss Scarlett, Reverend Green, Mrs Peacock, Professor Plum and Mrs White would all be in the same ownership. Never mind.

Miss Scarlett and Mrs White failed to score but Mrs Peacock and the Reverend Green were winners and during the 1970s and early 1980s, Colonel Mustard and Professor Plum won a dozen races each for trainer Captain Tim Forster. They murdered the opposition (sorry).

A different Colonel Mustard won three times on the Flat between 1998 and 2001. There may have been other horses with the same names in years gone by but I'll leave those for you to find. It's no job for the elderly.

> **Colonel Mustard:** 'Just checking.'
> **Mrs Peacock:** 'Everything all right?'
> **Colonel Mustard:** 'Yep. Two corpses. Everything's fine.'
> *From the 1985 film* Clue, *based on Cluedo*

Jolly bad names

Businessman (2007)
• *Acclamation* • *Venus Rising (Observatory)*
Not a name that captures the romance and excitement of horseracing. Even so, he won on his debut at York in 2009 before being fatally injured on his next run.

Ebitda (2014)
• *Compton Place* • *Tipsy Girl (Haafhd)*
A terrible name to inflict on a living creature. Ebitda is the accountancy term for earnings before interest, tax, depreciation and amortisation. She overcame her name to win six times in 2017.

Totopoly

The horseracing board game launched by Waddingtons in 1938 recruited the dozen most recent winners of the Lincoln Handicap for its field of horses.

So King Of Clubs (1926), Priory Park (1927), Dark Warrior (1928), Elton (1929), Leonidas II (1930), Knight Error (1931), Jerome Fandor (1932), Dorigen (1933), Play On (1934), Flamenco (1935),

Overcoat (1936) and Marmaduke Jinks (1937) lived on.

More jolly bad names

Nato (1972)

• *Prince de Galles* • *Miss Atlanta (Hethersett)*

The dam offers some excuse but even so ... The North Atlantic Treaty Organization failed on the racecourse, giving up without a fight after a few fruitless sallies as a two-year-old.

Nafta (1992)

• *Music Boy* • *Single Bid (Auction Ring)*

The acronym for the North American Free Trade Agreement failed to win in 14 attempts during 1994 and 1995.

6. CHARACTERS

Andy Pandy was a rather drippy, striped-pyjama-clad puppet who, from 1950, lived in a picnic basket on BBC Television. His friends Looby Loo, a rag doll, and Teddy, a teddy bear, weren't any better. Many children loved them but I thought Rag, Tag and Bobtail and The Flowerpot Men were better.

Andy Pandy became more manly in the 1970s. Paddy Mullins trained him to win three hurdle races and four chases in Ireland in 1975/76, before the seven-year-old moved to England to join Fred Rimell.

Sandwiched between victory in a Grand National Trial at Haydock and in the 1977 Whitbread Gold Cup, Andy Pandy started as favourite for that year's Grand National. Powering along a dozen lengths clear approaching Becher's Brook for the second time, Andy Pandy buckled on landing and fell, leaving Red Rum to claim his record-breaking third Grand National success.

> Time to go home, time to go home,
> Andy is waving goodbye.
> *Good. The regular finale to* Andy Pandy *on the BBC in the 1950s and 1960s*

Races won: 1977 Whitbread Gold Cup, plus three hurdles and three other chases from 1975 to 1977.

LOOBY LOO (2006)
• Kyllachy • Halland Park Lass (Spectrum)

Tried her luck as a racehorse in 2009 but gave up after
two attempts.

ANTON CHIGURH (2009)
• Oasis Dream • Barathiki (Barathea)

If the horse is anything like the character in Cormac McCarthy's
2005 novel *No Country for Old Men* and the Coen Brothers' 2007
film of the same title, you would not want him in your stable.
Hopefully the equine version, lodged at Nikki Evans's yard,
is better behaved.

Played in the film with chilling effect by Javier Bardem,
Chigurh is an emotionless, psychopathic hitman whose first
reaction on meeting another human being tends to be to toss
a coin to decide whether or not to kill them, and then kill them.

Anton Chigurh the horse has been less lethal, winning six times
on the Flat between 2012 and 2016. Five of the wins have been for
trainer Tom Dascombe and owner Panarea Racing, who are keen
on either the book, the film, or the mentally deranged.

> **Anton Chigurh:** 'Call it.'
> **Carla Jean Moss:** 'No. I ain't gonna call it.'
> **Anton Chigurh:** 'Call it.'
> **Carla Jean Moss:** 'The coin don't have no say.
> It's just you.'
> **Anton Chigurh:** 'Well, I got here the same way
> the coin did.'
> No Country For Old Men, *2007*

Races won: six small ones.

Traitorous names

Quisling (1961)
• *High Treason* • *Lake Lavandou (Le Lavandou)*
Unlike his namesake, he was never Head of the Norwegian
Government. On the other hand, he won ten races and wasn't shot
at the end of the Second World War.

Traitor (1970)
• *Quisling* • *Hindlight (Borealis)*
Won twice in 1972 and 1973.

Collaborator (1972)
• *Quisling* • *Bright and Breezy (Set Fair)*
Collaborating didn't do him any good. He failed to win in 24 attempts
from 1974 to 1977.

BIGGLES (1978)
• Derring-Do • Progress (March Past)

Only the death of author Captain WE Johns in 1968 put an end to
Biggles, although some local councils, librarians and schools had
already removed him from their shelves on the grounds of racism,
sexism and violence. If there'd been a statue of Biggles it might well
have been taken down.

A heroic pilot, Biggles flew in almost 100 books, many of them to
take on the Germans in the First and Second World Wars and tackle
baddies all over the world. Biggles was a bestseller, with generations of
schoolboys lapping up his derring-do. Later, as an outdated character
with outdated attitudes, Biggles became a figure of derision and fun.

In 1972, an episode of *Monty Python's Flying Circus* was titled
'Biggles Dictates a Letter'. He doesn't come out of it well and the
scene ends with the promise (unfulfilled) of another episode,
to be called 'Biggles Flies Undone'.

'I shall have to knock this fellow on the skull.'
Biggles in Captain WE Johns' Biggles in the Baltic *(1940)*

Biggles (Graham Chapman): 'Miss Bladder, take a letter.'
Secretary (Nicki Howorth): 'Yes, Señor Biggles.'
Biggles: 'Don't call me señor! I'm not a Spanish person.
You must call me Mr Biggles, or Group Captain Biggles,
or Mary Biggles if I'm dressed as my wife, but never señor.'
'Biggles Dictates a Letter' in 'Salad Days' episode of Monty
Python's Flying Circus, *1972*

Races won: on the racecourse, Biggles failed to get off the ground,
giving up after three goes as a two-year-old. The real Biggles would
never have given up.

BILLY BUNTER (1989)
* Nicholas Bill * Cosset (Comedy Star)

'Oh, crikey!' exclaimed the Fat Owl of the Remove as Lieutenant-
Commander George Gosselin Marten DSC, known to his friends
as 'Toby', told Billy Bunter that, now that he was Marten's
racehorse, there would be no more cake.

Like so much in life, it depends on when you were born. Marten
was born in 1918, which meant that his childhood and adolescence
encountered Billy Bunter, the fat, greedy, lazy schoolboy
responsible for the *Magnet's* popularity between 1908 and 1940.
Later, in the 1950s, Billy Bunter of Greyfriars School, played
perfectly by Gerald Campion, moved to television.

Marten, who bred and owned Billy Bunter, had several horses
in training with Henry Candy and David Elsworth, notably Dead
Certain, a high-class filly who won the 1989 Group 1 Cheveley
Park Stakes.

Marten had other claims to fame. During the Second World
War, he commanded the escort destroyer HMS *Wilton*, named
after the Wilton Hunt, and was awarded the Distinguished Service

Cross for gallantry. Later, he became naval equerry to King George VI, who attended Marten's 1949 wedding to Mary Sturt, the only child of the 3rd Lord Alington.

When Alington died, in 1940, Mary inherited the Crichel Estate in Dorset. Two years earlier, over 700 acres of the estate had been requisitioned for RAF bombing practice. After the war, despite Winston Churchill's wartime promise that former owners would be offered their land back, the Ministry of Agriculture and Commissioners of Crown Land installed a tenant. What followed became known as the Crichel Down affair.

Toby and Mary Marten launched a campaign that led, in 1954, to a public inquiry, a highly critical report by Sir Andrew Clark QC and the resignation of Sir Thomas Dugdale, the Minister of Agriculture. The land was restored to Mary Marten.

> 'I say, you fellows, that beastly postal order's got to be found,' gasped Bunter.
> *Frank Richards (a pen name of Charles Hamilton),* Billy Bunter's Postal Order, *1951. Bunter was forever awaiting a postal order from relatives.*

Races won: given his gluttony and the size of his girth, Billy Bunter was ill-equipped to win races. He didn't, falling back exhausted after eight tries in 1992 and 1993.

BESSIE BUNTER (1996)
• Rakaposhi King • Black H'Penny (Town and Country)

Billy Bunter's sister went to Cliff House School for Girls, making her magazine debut in *The School Friend* in 1919. Initially, the stories were written by Charles Hamilton under the pen name of Hilda Richards.

Unfortunately, from a racing point of view, Bessie was as greedy and fat as her brother. That was doubtless responsible for her failure to win in nine races under Rules in 2002 and 2003 but she was kept away from the kitchen long enough to win three point-to-point races during the following two years.

Yummy (2013)
• *Candy Ride* • *Moments of Joy (Lost Code)*
Bought for $5,000 as a yearling, Yummy hasn't raced. Maybe she's been eaten.
    There are other Yummys, but none with pedigrees suggesting they are yummy.

Yummy With Butter (2004)
• *Silvador* • *Sophisticatedbagel (Kris S.)*
Went down well, winning seven races between 2007 and 2012, five at Woodbine and two Grade 3 races at Monmouth Park.

Yummy In Da Tummy (2003)
• *Northern Spur* • *Waltzing Camel (Sheikh Albadou)*
A lesser Yummy, failing to win in 14 attempts between 2005 and 2007.

Blackadder and Company

The popularity of the *Blackadder* television comedy series in the 1980s and beyond seeped into the racing community, as you are about to read, if you haven't got anything better to do. You probably haven't.

BLACKADDER (2012)
• Myboycharlie • Famcred (Inchinor)

A huge popular success in his several roles, Edmund Blackadder's attempt to be a racehorse failed miserably. There's still time, but from 2014 to 2018, Blackadder failed to win in 31 attempts. On the other hand ...

BLACK ADDER (2000)
• Sire unregistered • Dam unregistered (Dam's sire unknown)

The first series was called *The Black Adder* and, in its honour, a horse was named Black Adder. His was an unpromising birth, neither his sire nor dam being registered in the General Stud Book.

Never mind, Black Adder joined the army, the King's Troop Royal Horse Artillery, and in 2010 won a special point-to-point at Larkhill – the King's Troop RHA Club Members' race. Black Adder had been runner-up the year before and was runner-up the year after. Well done.

> Field Marshal Haig is about to make yet another gargantuan effort to move his drinks cabinet six inches closer to Berlin.
> Blackadder Goes Forth, *1989. The best series in the Blackadder oeuvre*

BALDRICK (2000)
• Sire unregistered • Dam unregistered (Dam's sire unknown)

Baldrick was the hapless, hopeless butt of Blackadder's withering contempt. Unsurprisingly, his sire and dam were not registered in the General Stud Book. This would have been of some comfort to Blackadder, although he would have been horrified to discover that Baldrick had followed Black Adder into the King's Troop Royal Horse Artillery.

Fittingly, when both contested the 2009 RHA Club Members' race at Larkhill, while Black Adder finished second, Baldrick unseated his rider.

PRIVATE BALDRICK (2013)
• Captain Gerrard • Wingasinga (Black Hawk)

Private Baldrick had more luck in Australia, winning his first two races in 2017 for trainer Alexander Rae. Admittedly, he lost the next nine.

They weren't big races, Private Baldrick's victories being at Hanging Rock, which races on only two days a year, and Stony Creek. Still, they're racetracks with nice names.

> **Blackadder:** 'Baldrick, what are you doing out there?'
> **Baldrick:** 'I'm carving something on a bullet, sir.'
> **Blackadder:** 'What are you carving?'
> **Baldrick:** 'I'm carving "Baldrick", sir. You know how they say that somewhere there's a bullet with your name on it?'
> **Blackadder:** 'Yyyyyes...'
> **Baldrick:** 'Well, I thought that if I owned the bullet with my name on it, I'll never get hit by it! 'Cause I'll never shoot myself.'
> Blackadder Goes Forth, *1989*

FLASHHEART (2010)
• Nayef • Emerald Peace (Green Desert)

Very loud, very brash and a great admirer of himself, Lord Flashheart was played to the hilt by Rik Mayall. On the racecourse he was less heroic, winning just one small race at Chepstow in 2013.

> Hey, queenie! You look sexy. Listen, wear your hair long, I prefer it that way.
> Blackadder II, *1986*

LORD FLASHEART (1997)
* Blush Rambler • Miss Henderson Co (Silver Hawk)

It probably should be Flashheart but it wouldn't have mattered to Squadron Commander The Lord Flashheart, whose bombast swept all before him.

The self-proclaimed ace pilot and sex god wouldn't have been surprised that he won five races in France, including a Group 3 race at Longchamp in 1999 and the Group 2 Prix Hocquart at Chantilly in 2000. 'Flash' would have been more surprised that he was only second in that year's Prix du Jockey Club.

> Mind if I use your phone? If word gets out I'm missing, five
> hundred girls will kill themselves and I wouldn't want them
> on my conscience, not when they ought to be on my face!
> Blackadder Goes Forth, *1989*

GENERAL MELCHETT (2007)
* Broadway Flyer • Kept In The Dark (Kemal)

Also played to the hilt by Stephen Fry, General Melchett was a loud, stupid, domineering First World War army officer indifferent to the lethal consequences of sending men over the top of the trenches.

His career as a racehorse was short, comprising two National Hunt Flat races in 2011, in which he finished a creditable third and second.

> If nothing else works, a total pig-headed unwillingness
> to look facts in the face will see us through.
> Blackadder Goes Forth, *1989*

MRS MIGGINS (2013)
* Presenting • Carrigeen Lunaria (Saddlers' Hall)

Owner Barry Wright is a fan of *Blackadder* and that is why the mare he has with David Pipe is called Mrs Miggins.

Played by the splendidly named Helen Atkinson-Wood, the similarly splendid Mrs Miggins owns a pie shop and coffee shop, the setting for several amusing scenes in *Blackadder the Third*.

> **Mrs Miggins**: 'Bonjour, monsieur.'
> **Blackadder**: 'What?'
> **Mrs Miggins**: 'Bonjour, monsieur. It's French.'
> **Blackadder**: 'So is eating frogs, cruelty to geese and urinating in the street, but that's no reason to inflict it on the rest of us!'
> Blackadder the Third, *1987*

Races won: give her a chance – she didn't have her first race until 2018. So far she has twice finished third, from three attempts.

QUEENIE (1998)
* Indian Ridge • Bint Zamayem (Rainbow Quest)

Played brilliantly by Miranda Richardson, Queen Elizabeth I was portrayed as an unpredictable childlike maniac, prone to threats of execution.

> **Queen**: 'Oh, Edmund, I do love it when you get cross. Sometimes I think about having you executed just to see the expression on your face.'
> Blackadder II, *1986*

Races won: internationally there have been several Queenies. The British one won a maiden race at Chester in 2001 and that was all.

STRANGELY BROWN (2001)
* Second Empire • Damerela (Alzao)

One for Blackadder addicts. In the final episode of *Blackadder*, George (played by Hugh Laurie) mentions that Strangely Brown was the nickname of one of his schoolmates. They all had nicknames and they were all killed in the First World War.

Strangely Brown fared much better as a racehorse. Having won three times on the Flat for trainer Stuart Williams, he was bought as a three-year-old by Irish trainer Eric McNamara for 11,000 guineas and, racing for the We Didn't Name Him syndicate, promptly won his first three hurdle races. The syndicate had struck gold with a high-class hurdler who won over £200,000 for them.

> **Blackadder**: 'How are all the boys now?'
> **George**: 'Bumfluff copped a packet at Gallipoli with the Aussies. So did Drippy and Strangely Brown. Gosh, I suppose I'm the only one of the Trinity Tiddlers still alive.'
> *'Goodbyeee', the final episode of* Blackadder *and arguably the best, 1989*

Races won: 2005 Grade 1 Prix Alain Du Breil at Auteuil, Grade 2 Cashmans Juvenile Hurdle and a Grade 3 hurdle; 2016 Listed hurdle at Aintree.

BUZZ LIGHTYEAR (1996)
• Gold Brose • Excitable Kid (Youth)

'To infinity and beyond!' was the catchphrase of Buzz Lightyear, the star toy space ranger in *Toy Story* (1995), a wonderfully innovative computer-generated cartoon film with the bonus of music by Randy Newman.

A year later, in New Zealand, Buzz Lightyear reappeared in the form of a horse. Although the equine space ranger didn't reach infinity or beyond, he did go on to win the 1999 New Zealand 2,000 Guineas and Bayer Classic in the colours of Test cricketer Terry Jarvis before running out of stamina in the Sleepyhead New Zealand Derby.

Subsequently, there was a *Buzz Lightyear (2009)* in Sweden, who won twice there in 2011 and later still there was a Buzz Lightyere in England. In 2017, trained by Philip Hide and owned by the Tara Moon Partnership, *Buzz Lightyere (2013)* won three times, accompanied by a supporter wearing a terrific Buzz Lightyear costume. In 2018, he won again.

> You got troubles, I've got 'em too
> There isn't anything I wouldn't do for you
> We stick together and see it through
> Cause you've got a friend in me.
> *Randy Newman, 'You've Got a Friend in Me'. The theme song
> for* Toy Story *and its sequels*

Races won: 1999 New Zealand 2,000 Guineas, Bayer Classic, New Zealand Derby Trial.

An absolutely splendid name

Hewouldwouldnthe (2014)

* *Sixties Icon* ● *Gib (Rock Of Gibraltar)*

An icon of sorts, Mandy Rice-Davies was more than merely a focus of sexual curiosity as a player in the Profumo Affair. That's the one that, in 1963, led to minister John Profumo's resignation from the Conservative government.

Rice-Davies may have been blonde but she was not dumb. When a barrister pointed out that Lord Astor denied her claim to have had an affair with him she retorted, memorably, 'Well, he would, wouldn't he?' Rice-Davies used her notoriety and bright personality to help forge a successful career as an actress and businesswoman. As she put it, her post-Profumo life was 'one slow descent into respectability'.

Races won: one so far – an amateur riders' race at Wolverhampton in 2018, at 40-1.

CAPTAIN PUGWASH (2014)
• Sir Prancealot • Liscoa (Foxhound)

I bet you wish you were 70, so that your childhood could have embraced the jolly theme tune and seafaring larks of *Captain Pugwash* on BBC Television.

The theme tune was a catchy number played on the accordion to introduce the adventures of the not very evil – well, not evil at all – pirate Captain Horatio Pugwash and his not very bloodthirsty crew on the *Black Pig*.

Captain Pugwash first appeared in the *Eagle* magazine (see Dan Dare below) in 1950 and, from 1957 to 1966, in a cardboard-cut-out animation on the telly. There was another series in 1974/75 and a revival in 1997.

Tom the cabin boy was the clever one, forever saving Pugwash from a fate if not worse than death then death at the hands of the horrible Cut-Throat Jake (see below again).

While Tom was using his brains, Pugwash was exclaiming 'Blistering barnacles!' and 'Kipper me capstans!' It was all very jolly.

Captain Pugwash was revived again in 2014, in the form of a racehorse who won at Chelmsford three times in 2017 and 2018.

Stuttering starfish, what a staggering storm!
Captain Pugwash in 'Down the Hatch', 1974

Races won: three so far.

A Freudian name

Weareagrandmother (1987)
• *Prince Tenderfoot* • *Lady Bettina (Bustino)*

Sir Clement Freud named and initially owned Weareagrandmother after a royally worded announcement by Prime Minister Margaret Thatcher.

We have become a grandmother of a grandson.
Margaret Thatcher, March 1989

Races won: two on the Flat and two over hurdles 1989 to 1991.

CHRISTOPHER ROBIN (1996)
• Mac's Imp • Miss Ming (Tender King)

---

and

CHRISTOPHER ROBIN (2015)
• Camelot • Iowa Falls (Dansili)

The young boy in AA Milne's stories and poems featuring Winnie-the-Pooh brought pleasure to literally millions of children but a lot of personal misery to Milne's son, on whom the character was based.

As a racehorse, Christopher Robin was much less successful than the books he appeared in. The one whose career under Rules consisted of three poor efforts as a two-year-old in 1998 had some excuse, having cost only 3,000 guineas, but the one who so far has scored one from seven needs to do a lot better to justify his price of 400,000 guineas.

They're changing guard at Buckingham Palace
Christopher Robin went down with Alice.
AA Milne, When We Were Very Young *(1924)*

You probably need a break. I know I do.

Let's pause for breath.

CORPORAL CLINGER (1979)
• Bruni • Penny Candy (Tamerlane)

Or it could be Corporal (later Sergeant) Klinger. Let's not quibble over a letter. Either way he was that character in *M*A*S*H* who dressed as a woman in the hope of being discharged from the army as mentally unfit. It didn't work.

The television series was a spin-off from the 1970 film, *MASH*, which was inspired by a 1968 novel called *MASH*, by Richard Hooker. They were all based in a mobile army hospital unit during the Korean War.

While the war lasted three years (1950 to 1953), the television series lasted 11, from 1972 to 1983. It must have been a bit like working in *Coronation Street* but without Ena Sharples or Elsie Tanner. It's not my fault if you've never heard of them.

Wearing a bridle rather than a bridal dress, Corporal Clinger reappeared over jumps in 1983 and became a high-class hurdler for Martin Pipe. After winning the Bula Hurdle at Cheltenham

and the Swinton Hurdle at Haydock in 1985, Corporal Clinger
was made second favourite behind See You Then for the 1986
Champion Hurdle. It didn't stop him falling.

Corporal Clinger spent his old age with trainer Andrew Crook,
dying in 2012, aged 33.

> I've got a soft spot for Klinger. He looks a little like my son
> and he dresses a lot like my wife.
> *Colonel Potter,* M*A*S*H

Races won: After winning twice on the Flat in 1982, Corporal
Clinger won nine times over hurdles, including the 1985 Bula and
Swinton Hurdles, 1987 National Spirit Hurdle and 1988 Mecca
Bookmakers Hurdle.

A romantic name

Coeur Blimey (2011)
* Winged Love * Eastender (Opening Verse)
Very clever and not a bad racehorse, so far winning a Listed bumper
race at Ascot in 2015, a hurdle at Wetherby in 2017, and a Flat race
at Chepstow in 2018.

CUT THROAT JAKE (1997)
* Karinga Bay * French Lip (Scorpio)

A bloodthirsty pirate with a big black beard and an eye patch,
Cut-Throat Jake was the constant enemy of Captain Pugwash (see
above). Forever foiled in his dastardly plans by Tom the cabin boy,
in 2002 Cut-Throat Jake reappeared without the hyphen in Simon
Gilmore's Northamptonshire yard.

Owned, appropriately, by a racing syndicate called Pieces
Of Eight, Cut Throat Jake was as unsuccessful as his namesake,
running six times without winning.

You know what the likes of me does to the likes of you.
We makes you walk the plank; feed you to the fishes.
Cut-Throat Jake in 'The Plank', 1975

Races won: none.

A wobbly name

Waddle Home (1978)
• Duck Dance • Bender (Court Recess)
His name was probably the best thing about him because he may
never have raced. In 1984 Waddle Home was sold in New York for just
$900 as a 'racing prospect'. Hope springs eternal.

DAN DARE (1999)
• *Efisio* • *Daring Ditty (Daring March)*

and

DAN DARE (2003)
• Dynaformer • Etheldreda (Diesis)

Dan Dare, Pilot of the Future, lives on. The high-principled,
square-jawed hero of the *Eagle* magazine's famous space fiction strip
cartoon was reborn as a racehorse. Sent to Richard Hannon senior,
Dan Dare (1999) proved the palest possible shadow of his namesake,
running just three times, poorly.

As so often with Dan Dare, 'The World's Number One Space
Hero!', all was not lost. In 2003 an American-bred version
appeared on Earth and was bought at Keeneland for $425,000.
It was rather more than the space hero was worth but he did win
a maiden race at Newcastle for owner Philip Newton and trainer
Sir Michael Stoute before moving on to Noel Meade in Ireland,
where he won a maiden hurdle at Fairyhouse.

The world awaits a thoroughbred worthy of Dan Dare's name. He, his podgy assistant Digby and the rest of his spacecraft's crew starred in the *Eagle* from its first appearance in 1950 until 1967, with revivals from 1977 to 1979, 1982 to 1994 and beyond.

Without Dan Dare, the evil Mekon, sitting on a floating saucer, his huge green head full of malice, would have destroyed the human race long ago. When you consider what human beings do to each other, it may not have been a bad thing. It's about time someone named a horse The Mekon.

The Mekon: 'Enjoy your brief triumph, Dare! I shall return to destroy you and your kind!'
Dan Dare: 'Don't be so sure, Mekon! Death rides with you!'
Eagle, *'Prisoners of Space', 1954/55*

Races won: Dan Dare (GB), none. Dan Dare (USA), one on the Flat 2007, one hurdle 2008.

Breaking news: The Mekon (2015) appeared on Earth, at Redcar, in May 2018. Earthlings, beware!

Blasts of names

Whoomph (1971)
• *Blast* • *Avonella (Rockavon)*
Won four races in 1973 and 1974.

Whoosh (1971)
• *Blast* • *Conita (Constable)*
A non-winner.

DESPERATE DAN (2001)

● Danzero ● Alzianah (Alzao)

As Desperate Dan made his debut in the *Dandy* in 1937 and the magazine had a circulation of two million in the 1950s, there were probably equine reincarnations long before he won two Flat races as a two-year-old in 1973.

Yet no Desperate Dan could have been as prolific a winner as the one that ran 100 times from 2003 to 2011, winning 19 races along the way. They were humble contests, many of them selling and claiming races.

Jamie Osborne trained Desperate Dan for his first three triumphs but after winning a seller at Wolverhampton in 2007 the six-year-old was bought for 12,000 guineas by trainer Andy Haynes, who won another 16 races with him.

The comic character, brawny, big of chin, unshaven (he shaved with a blowtorch but it didn't seem to work) and devoted to enormous cow pies, was as strong as a horse and could lift a cow with one arm. It wasn't a talent useful for racing but Desperate Dan became an international thoroughbred. Between 2012 and 2016 an Australian version *(2007)* won seven races in New South Wales. So he wasn't just an ugly face.

> Say, boys, look at Dan sneezing. He's blown a hole
> in the floor!
> *Desperate Dan cartoon in* The Dandy

BERYL THE PERIL (1996)
● Presidium ● Vague Reply (Vaigly Great)

Another star name in the comic cosmos, first launched in the *Topper* in 1953, joining up with the *Beezer* in 1990, and finally recruited for the *Dandy* three years later.

Beryl started life as the schoolgirl counterpart of Dennis the Menace, a tearaway creator of havoc. Although Beryl never aged she calmed down over the years. She'll probably be going on mystery coach tours soon.

I'll hide in here. Then, when the others go into school,
I'll sneak off.
Beryl the Peril in The Topper

Races won: None. Proved hopeless three times in 1998 and 1999.
Was expelled after that.

A jolly bad name

Caravan Centre (1972)
• Nelcius • Princesse Moss (Mossborough)
A terrible name for a horse, and one that killed any hope of winning the
Derby or Oaks at baptism. She did win a selling race at Catterick in
1975, but there was no bid afterwards. Quite right too.

DICK BARTON (1976)
• St Alphage • Rijika (Ragusa)

Dick Barton, Special Agent. There's something engaging about the
title of the hugely popular radio programme which ran from 1946
to 1951, with various reincarnations.

The frenetic signature tune, 'Devil's Galop', set the tone perfectly
for the post-war adventures of Captain Richard Barton MC and his
sidekicks, Jock Anderson and Snowy White. Together they saved
civilisation from a string of dastardly criminals and spies. All was
regularly almost lost, only to be saved by implausible escapes.
The one thing Dick Barton could not escape was replacement
by *The Archers*. There aren't many master criminals in Ambridge.

With one bound he was free!
Dick Barton, daily

Races won: none. He only ran as a two-year-old and not fast enough. Perhaps he went to Madagascar and conquered the world there.

HORATIO HORNBLOWER (2008)
• Presenting • Countess Camilla (Bob's Return)

My Uncle Norman, who captained a motor torpedo boat in the Mediterranean during the Second World War and smoked a pipe, was a great fan of CS Forester's naval novels featuring Horatio Hornblower.

I don't know if Norman picked up any tips. Probably not, as Hornblower was fighting Napoleon while my uncle was taking on Hitler. Horatio and Norman both won.

As did Horatio Hornblower, who won five jumps races for trainer Nick Williams between 2012 and 2018.

> I'd rather be in trouble for having done something
> than for not having done anything.
> *Horatio Hornblower in* Lieutenant Hornblower
> *by CS Forester (1952)*

> Where's my pipe?
> *Uncle Norman, 1962*

LORD JIM (1961)
• Kelling • Jumping Powder (Foxhunter)

Strange to name a horse after a character in Joseph Conrad's novel who was racked with guilt and ends up being shot dead. Still, it didn't work out too badly on the racecourse. One Lord Jim won the Mandarin Chase in 1970, finished second in that year's Hennessy Gold Cup and won the 1971 National Hunt Chase at Cheltenham.

Another Lord Jim (1992), bred in Ireland, won four Flat and three hurdle races between 1995 and 2001, including a Listed race in Ireland, while a third Lord Jim (2009), also bred in Ireland, won a maiden race at Bellewstown in 2012. The later Lord Jim was allowed to be called Lord Jim because the 1992 Lord Jim had died more than five years earlier, which meant his name could be used again.

It may be worth naming your next horse Lord Jim.

It was a dark story.
Joseph Conrad, Lord Jim, *1900. It certainly was. No wonder Walt Disney didn't make the film.*

Races won: Lord Jim (the best one) won four jumps races including – well, I've already told you. You shouldn't need to be told twice.

Good names

Civil Servant (1972)
• *Frigid Aire* • *Pink Tape (Supreme Court)*
Rather clever. Won two small races in 1977.

Stolen Brief (1971)
• *Burglar* • *Lady Advocate (King's Bench)*
A non-winner, except on the naming front.

MAD JACK MYTTON (2010)
• Arcadio • Gilt Ridden (Heron Island)

Surprisingly, this character was real.

John, alias Jack, Mytton was born at Halston Hall in Shropshire in 1796. Two years later his father died, leaving Jack an enormous estate with a huge annual income to look forward to. Unfortunately, by the time he inherited it, he had already spent a lot of it.

Expelled from Westminster School for fighting a master, Mytton failed to stay the course at Harrow before arriving at Cambridge University with no academic intent but dedicated to the 2,000 bottles of port he reputedly brought with him.

Mytton was so keen on horses that he put one in a tutor's bedroom and gave another, named Sportsman, a bottle of mulled port, with fatal consequences.

Mytton sometimes rode naked in the tradition of Lady Godiva and in 1826 rode a horse into a hotel, a venture later copied by the Irish trainer Oliver Brady. In 2009 Brady led Pablo, the winner of the 2003 Lincoln, into the ballroom of the Glencarn Hotel in Castleblayney to liven up a Cheltenham Festival preview.

In Mytton's case it was the Bedford Hotel in Leamington Spa, a centre of the hunting fraternity. Mad Jack rode Mad Tom up the grand staircase and into the first-floor dining room, where he jumped over both tables and diners.

That was a small sample of Mytton's madnesses. According to 'Thormanby' in *Famous Racing Men* (1882), 'the most lenient view to take of his character is that he was insane and not responsible for his actions'.

It didn't help that he was in a 'nearly constant state of intoxication' and 'for the last twelve years of his life it may safely be stated that he was never sober'. As he drank between four and six bottles of port a day, later succeeded in his affections by brandy, it was not surprising. Nor was the fact that Mytton's first wife died young and his second wife fled.

By then the money had run out and in 1831 Mytton moved to France to escape his creditors, returning in 1833 to die a year later in a debtors' prison.

Sir Thomas Burgh's escapades, of both the Mytton and the Casanova kind, were notorious.
Mad Jack still remembered, in John Fowles's, The French Lieutenant's Woman *(1969)*

Races won: Mad Jack Mytton won four times over jumps between 2013 and 2017.

NICHOLAS NICKLEBY (1951)
● Niccolo Dell'Arca ● Grande Corniche (Panorama)

Charles Dickens wrote a very successful novel about him and over 100 years later Nicholas Nickleby staged a fruitful comeback as a racehorse.

In 1955, ridden by Willie Snaith and trained by Sam Armstrong, Nicholas Nickleby won the Royal Hunt Cup at 50-1 and in 1958, ridden by Joe Mercer, won the Newbury Spring Cup.

In Dickens's novel, Nicholas Nickleby's sister is called Kate but in his equine reincarnation Nicholas's sister was *Bebe Grande (1950)*, winner of the 1952 Gimcrack Stakes, Champagne Stakes and Cheveley Park Stakes. The following year Bebe Grande finished second in the 2,000 Guineas and, two days later, was third in the 1,000 Guineas.

As well as being a horse, Bebe Grande was also the world's largest fibreglass yacht, owned, like the horse and Nicholas Nickleby, by 'Lucky' Jack Gerber. Gerber was a wealthy South African steel magnate and gambler who also owned *By Thunder! (1951)*, winner of the 1954 Ebor Handicap and 1955 Yorkshire Cup.

Gerber kept dubious company, including that of London gang leader Billy Hill. On meeting Hill, Gerber once bravely or foolishly said, 'Ah, Mr Hill, murdered anyone recently?'

> A horse is a quadruped, and quadruped's Latin for beast,
> as everybody that's gone through the grammar knows,
> or else where's the use of having grammars at all?
> *Wackford Squeers in* Nicholas Nickleby

Races won: Nicholas Nickleby won 12 races, notably the 1955 Royal Hunt Cup and 1958 Newbury Spring Cup.

Names that won't do

Boardroom (1971)
• *Lauso* • *Seat in the Sun (King's Bench)*
Slight mitigation on account of the dam's name, but calling a horse Boardroom? Naaah! Disadvantaged at his naming ceremony, he managed to win three times on the Flat in 1973 and 1974.

Shop Steward (1974)
• *Fleece* • *Heron's Strike (Combat)*
Perhaps the name was prompted by the pedigree. Even so ... Hopeless.

Tennis Ball (1974)
• *Charlottown* • *Some Tune (Tin Whistle)*
Hopeless in 1976 and failed to bounce back in 1977; then gave up.

OUTLAW JOSEY WALES (2011)
• Jeremy • Trinity Scholar (Invincible Spirit)

The horse's last name was Wales, and so was that of part-owner William Wright Wales, who had a long-established butcher's business in Kilmarnock and also sang for the Ayr Intimate Opera.

Clint Eastwood directed as well as starred in *The Outlaw Josey Wales*, set in and after the American Civil War. It was one of a string of terrific Westerns that helped make Eastwood's name, from Sergio Leone's 'spaghetti' Westerns of the 1960s to perhaps his best, which Eastwood also directed, *Unforgiven* (1992). Sadly, Billy Wales died in 2016, after his horse had raced only twice.

> **Captain Fletcher:** 'I think I'll try to tell him the war is over. What do you say, Mr Wilson?'
> **Josey Wales (alias Mr Wilson):** 'I reckon so. I guess we all died a little in that damn war.'

The closing lines of *The Outlaw Josey Wales*. Fletcher knows

that Mr Wilson is Josey Wales and that he has not been killed
in Mexico, as friends claimed, but chooses to let him be.

> Not many toreadors have to be taken to hospital before
> they tackle the bull, but that's what happened to Billy
> Wales, who plays Escamillo the toreador in Ayr Intimate
> Opera's production of *Carmen*. Disaster struck when Billy
> recently cut his thumb on a meat-cutting machine.
> Ayrshire Post, *September 1977*

Races won: none so far.

PC DIXON (2013)
 • Sixties Icon • Lakaam (Danzero)

Police Constable George Dixon was unique. When every other
policeman was retiring, Dixon of Dock Green was just starting.

Actor Jack Warner was already 60 when the first episode of the
iconic television series was broadcast, in 1955. By the time the final
episode was reached, an amazing 21 years later, Warner was 80.

There were no *Sweeney*-type chases or violence; either would have
killed Warner. Instead, each episode – there were over 400 of them
– began with the homely Dixon ambling out of the police station to
stand under a police lamp, touch his helmet and say, 'Evening, all.'

After a gentle encounter with local petty criminals, all was well,
and Dixon again stood beneath the police lamp to say farewell:
'Goodnight, all.' In 1955 he said it in black and white, but from 1969
he said it in colour.

Mick Channon bred and initially owned PC Dixon, but after
ten abortive efforts handed the truncheon to Victor Thompson for
£5,500. In 2018, on his nineteenth try, PC Dixon finally entered
a winner's enclosure, at Hexham at 33-1. If you'd kept faith you'd
have shown a level stake profit.

Races won: just the one, so far. PC Dixon isn't one to give up.

PRISONER OF ZENDA (1972)
• Manacle • Ruritania (Pampered King)

A rollicking adventure, Anthony Hope's late nineteenth-century bestseller made the fictional Ruritania better known than a lot of real countries – Togo, for instance – and Ruritania lasted longer than many countries.

As so often, the most captivating character is a baddie, Rupert of Hentzau. Hope was sensible enough to keep him alive, ready for the sequel bearing his name (see below).

Good families are generally worse than any others.
Lady Rose Burlesdon in Anthony Hope, The Prisoner of Zenda *(1894)*

For my part, if a man must needs be a knave, I would have him a debonair knave, and I liked Rupert of Hentzau better than his long-faced, close-eyed companions. It makes your sin no worse, as I conceive, to do it a la mode and stylishly.
Anthony Hope, The Prisoner of Zenda *(1894)*

Races won: better at being rescued from prison than from outrunning his racecourse rivals, which he succeeded in doing only once, over hurdles at Bangor in 1981.

Tied up names

Manacle (1964)
• *Sing Sing* • *Hard and Fast (Hard Sauce)*
A prolific winner of 11 races between 1966 and 1968 before becoming a prolific stallion.

Fettered (1974)
• *Manacle* • *Anatevka (Privy Councillor)*

Despite his handicap, managed to win four times between 1976 and 1981.

Shackle (1972)
• *Manacle* • *Aberystwyth (Abernant)*
Wasn't hampered too badly as he won twice as a juvenile.

Handycuff (1972)
• *Manacle* • *Black Rage (My Babu)*
Fist fights and manacles couldn't slow him down. He won nine times on the Flat between 1974 and 1981, relishing mud, and three times over hurdles.

RUPERT OF HENTZAU (1999)
• Superpower • Walkonthemoon (Coquelin)

Dashing as a villain in *The Prisoner of Zenda* but distinctly undashing as a racehorse. After flopping eight times in a row as a two-year-old, Rupert of Hentzau was sold for a derisory £350, raising fears for his future. With Rupert's usual good luck, he became someone's well-loved pet.

> Among the sins of Rupert of Hentzau I do not assign the first and greatest place to his killing of the King. It was, indeed, the act of a reckless man who stood at nothing and held nothing sacred.
> *Anthony Hope,* Rupert of Hentzau *(1898). The sequel to* The Prisoner of Zenda

---

PRUFROCK (2014)
• *Roderic O'Connor* • *Indaba (Indian Ridge)*

That would be J. Alfred Prufrock, the fictitious subject of TS Eliot's poem *'The Love Song of J. Alfred Prufrock'*.

Prufrock was a bit of a mess, so it was asking a lot of him to pull himself together sufficiently to make a go of things as a racehorse, especially as he was required to cope with a sex change and race as a filly.

Maybe owner Dr Marcella Burns is a fan of TS Eliot and although Prufrock failed to score in seven runs in 2016 and 2017, he lives on in a cracking poem.

> Let us go then, you and I,
> When the evening is spread out against the sky
> Like a patient etherized upon a table.
> *The famous opening lines of TS Eliot's* 'The Love Song of J. Alfred Prufrock' *(1915). It includes other famous lines.*

Burglars' names

House Breaker (1974)
* Burglar • Leonora's Legend (Rockefella)
Stole a race (sorry) at Leicester as a two-year-old.

Swag (1972)
* Burglar • Stephanie (Souverain)
Failed to escape with any.

Thief (1974)
* Burglar • Lovely One (Ballymoss)
A failed one.

SADIE THOMPSON (2002)
* King's Best • Femme Fatale (Fairy King)

In 1916 the author William Somerset Maugham (1874–1965) sailed to American Samoa with his companion Gerald Haxton. Detained in the capital, Pago Pago, the pair shared a lodging house with another passenger, a Miss Thompson. Miss Thompson had taken a Samoan lover and Maugham was irritated by their noisy bedroom activities.

Five years later, along with other characters based on fellow passengers, Miss Thompson appeared as a prostitute in a short story named after her.

In 1928, Gloria Swanson starred as Sadie Thompson in a silent movie of that name. Controversially risqué at the time, the film was a considerable success, more so than both the 1932 version, called *Rain* and starring Joan Crawford, and the 1953 musical *Miss Sadie Thompson*, starring Rita Hayworth.

Today, visitors to Pago Pago can stay at the Sadie Thompson Inn, although she is no longer there.

> She was twenty-seven perhaps, plump, and in a coarse fashion pretty. She wore a white dress and a large white hat. Her fat calves in white cotton stockings bulged over the tops of long white boots in glacé kid.
> 'It's not the woman who was dancing with the quartermaster last night?' asked Mrs Davidson.
> 'That's who it must be,' said Mrs Macphail.
> 'I wondered at the time what she was. She looked rather fast to me.'
> *W. Somerset Maugham,* Miss Thompson *(title later changed to* Rain*) (1921)*

Races won: raced only twice, winning a maiden race at Warwick in 2004.

Avoiding names

Buzz Off (1958)
• *March Past* • *Too Much Honey (Honeyway)*
A specialist in selling races, Buzz Off won five of them between 1960 and 1964.

Shun (1972)

• *March Past* • *Louisine (Blue Peter)*
Shunned after two unpromising runs as a two-year-old.

SHERLOCK HOLMES (1986)
• Sexton Blake • Game Joan (Assagai)

Now there's a funny thing (see Max Miller in the next section). Sherlock Holmes, the great detective, was the son of Sexton Blake, another great fictional detective.

Sexton Blake (coming up next) appeared on the scene just as Sherlock Holmes appeared to have left it. In December 1893, Sexton Blake made his debut in a story called 'The Missing Millionaire' in the *Halfpenny Marvel* comic. The same month, in 'The Adventure of the Final Problem' in the *Strand* magazine, readers were led to believe that Holmes had fallen to his death at the Reichenbach Falls in a struggle with his arch enemy, Professor Moriarty.

However, we had not heard the last of either Sherlock Holmes, who rose again in 1903, or Moriarty.

In 1986 Mrs Teresa Moriarty – doubtless a descendant of the master criminal – was the owner of Sherlock Holmes!

It was an extraordinary act of revenge. Sherlock Holmes was in terrible danger. Having won on his debut at Kempton in 1988, Sherlock Holmes vanished.

How Moriarty must have gloated! Yet Holmes was not so easily disposed of. Years later he popped up again, this time in Ireland, posing as *Sherlock Holmes (2012)*. Having won twice there in 2015, Sherlock Holmes emigrated to Australia, so far winning three times there in 2017 and 2018.

He is the Napoleon of crime, Watson. He is the organiser of half that is evil and of nearly all that is undetected in this great city.

Sherlock Holmes of Professor Moriarty in Arthur Conan Doyle's 'The Adventure of the Final Problem' (1893)

CONAN DOYLE (1977)
• Derring-Do • Shot Gold (Vimy)

Having won once in 1979 and again in 1980, Conan Doyle was sold for 20,000 guineas and sent off to America. Just as it is hard to imagine Sherlock Holmes in New York, so it was with Conan Doyle. In four runs in 1982 he failed to solve the puzzle and earned just $450.

He should have stayed in England.

SEXTON BLAKE (1975)
• Blakeney • Mayo Blues (Abernant)

---

and

SEXTON BLAKE (2013)
• *Rip Van Winkle* • *Soviet Treat (Ashkalani)*

Like Sherlock Holmes but less regularly, Sexton Blake smoked a pipe, lived in Baker Street and always got his man (or woman). On the other hand, whereas Conan Doyle had a monopoly on Sherlock Holmes stories, Sexton Blake's exploits were written by several authors over a long period of time. Most weren't as good as Conan Doyle, at least until spiritualism got the better of him.

As a horse, Sexton Blake came in at least two forms, born in 1975 and 2013. The former was a credit to his namesake while the latter wasn't.

During the race, Blake discovered the owner of the favourite lying dead upon the turf.
A murder during the 1,000 Guineas, in 'The Great "Tote" Fraud', The Sexton Blake Library *(1929)*

Races won: the 1975 version won five races between 1977 and 1979, including the 1977 Group 2 Champagne Stakes and three Group 3 races. The 2013 model was winless in 13 races between 2015 and 2017.

7. PERFORMERS

ACKER BILK (2014)
• Rip Van Winkle • Portentous (Selkirk)

Which reminds me, if anyone's got my *The Best of Ball, Barber and Bilk* record from 1962, can I have it back, please?

Who can forget Acker Bilk's huge hit from the same year, 'Stranger on the Shore'? No one, surely, over the age of 70. Acker Bilk, Chris Barber, Kenny Ball, wonderful! Well, I liked them at the time. There was Acker Bilk with his goatee beard, striped waistcoat and bowler hat, playing the clarinet with his Paramount Jazz Band. Of course the Beatles, the Rolling Stones and the later 1960s arrived to make traditional jazz seem old-fashioned but Bilk bashed on, even though he got fed up of playing 'Stranger on the Shore'.

To give us all hope of resurrection, no sooner had Acker Bilk died, in 2014, than he rose again as a racehorse. What more proof do you need?

None.
'Stranger on the Shore' (1962). There weren't any words: it was an instrumental.

Races won: two so far, both in 2018.

An awful name

Sorry for interrupting your (hopefully) enjoyment by introducing ...

Bagapooh (2002)
• Bag • Mertzie Pooh (Mertzon).
The pedigree is a poor excuse. No wonder Bagapooh wasn't much good, racing 48 times but winning only a minor claiming race at Manor Downs in Texas in 2008. Manor Downs closed afterwards. My case rests.

ADORABLE CYRIL (1968)
• Royal Record • Swingtime (High Treason)

 In 1956 Cyril Stein, aged 28, bought Ladbrokes with his uncle for £100,000 and, taking the lead in exploiting the legalisation of betting shops in 1960, turned it into Britain's biggest bookmaker. In 1967 Ladbrokes was floated on the Stock Exchange at a valuation of £2 million. Stein was chairman from 1966 to 1993, by which time Ladbrokes was valued at over £2 billion.

While Stein was using advertising to good effect off-course, bookmaker John Banks was busy raising his profile on-course. He would arrive at a racecourse in a yellow Rolls-Royce, wearing his trademark black fedora hat and hand out ice creams, balloons and rosettes bearing the inscription, 'I Back with Banks'.

Banks enjoyed taunting Ladbrokes and punters enjoyed him doing it. In 1968 he applied to name a horse Greenwich Mean Stein. When the Jockey Club refused, Banks named it Adorable Cyril.

It was Banks, who also had a chain of shops in Glasgow, who famously remarked that betting shops were 'a licence to print money'. It was Stein who did most of the printing while, in 1978, Banks was warned off for three years for 'conduct likely to cause serious damage to the interests of horseracing'. That followed concern about his contacts with jockey John Francome.

The odds against winning consistently are 10,000 to 1.
I am the one.
John Banks

It's not just the best deal I've made, it's the best deal anyone has ever made.
Cyril Stein in 1991, when the chain of Hilton Hotels that Ladbrokes bought for £645 million in 1987 was valued at £2.5 billion.

Races won: 1970, two for John Banks; 1971, two for someone else.

Jukebox

Record Token (1972)
• *Jukebox* • *Bare Costs (Petition)*
Won nine times and played many good tunes, his finest when winning the Group 2 Vernons Sprint Cup at Haydock in 1976.

Slot Machine (1972)
• *Jukebox* • *Chandravati (Hard Tack)*
Living up to his name, took people's money but didn't give much back. On the other hand, he only operated for one season.

Whirlitzer (1972)
• *Jukebox* • *Gentle Katie (Anwar)*
Won twice, in 1975.

Music Boy (1973)
• *Jukebox* • *Veronique (Matador)*

A very fast two-year-old, winning the 1975 Windsor Castle Stakes at Royal Ascot and the Group 2 Gimcrack Stakes at York. The following year he won the Group 3 King George Stakes at Goodwood. Then he went to stud.

BLOSSOM DEARIE (1993)
• Landyap • Jose Collins (Singing Bede)

A great jazz singer and pianist but a poor racehorse. Never mind; if you have never heard Blossom Dearie's unique singing and playing then you've got at least one thing to look forward to.

She sang in a girlish, wryly amusing, observant voice; voice and piano in perfect, precise, partnership. There was no one like Blossom Dearie (1926–2009), and if you start with 'Peel Me a Grape', 'I'm Hip' and 'I'm Shadowing You' you'll discover how wonderful she was.

Now I'm deep into Zen meditation and macrobiotics
and, as soon as I can, I intend to get into narcotics.
Blossom Dearie, 'I'm Hip'

Here's how to be an agreeable chap
Love me and leave me in luxury's lap!
Hop when I holler, skip when I snap
When I say 'Do it!,' jump to it!
Blossom Dearie, 'Peel Me a Grape'

Races won: she should have won the 1,000 Guineas and Oaks, at least. Sadly, 11 tries on the Flat and over jumps from 1995 to 1998 were fruitless.

Likeable names

La Ville De Rire (1974)
• Town Crier • French Laughter (Gilles de Retz)
Was quite good and won four races in 1977 and 1978.

Press Luncheon (1971)
• Be Friendly • Twaddle (Tim Tam)
Won twice as a two-year-old in 1973.

Speculator (1971)
• Hopeful Venture • Pure Folly (Pandofell)
Won once in 1974.

BOBBY VEE (2014)
• Camacho • Miss Lesley (Needwood Blade)

You must remember – 'Rubber Ball', 'Take Good Care of My Baby', 'The Night Has a Thousand Eyes'. All big hits for Bobby Vee (1943–2016) in the early 1960s. It's not my fault if you weren't around then, have never heard of Bobby Vee or have been seduced by rap – dreadful stuff.

Two years before his death, Bobby Vee appeared as a filly, which was a bit odd, but it takes all sorts. Sadly, she didn't make much of an impression on the racecourse, winning just once, in 2016, from 14 attempts. She's still in training so maybe, like 'Rubber Ball', she'll 'come bouncin' back'.

> So, take good care of my baby
> Be just as kind as you can be
> And if you should discover
> That you don't really love her
> Just send my baby back home to me.
> *Bobby Vee, 'Take Good Care Of My Baby' (1961)*

Clever names to sing along with

Hay Chewed (2011)
• Camacho • Titian Saga (Titus Livius)
Won four races, including a Listed race at Ayr in 2014.
> Hey Jude, don't make it bad
> Take a sad song and make it better
> Remember to let her into your heart
> Then you can start to make it better.
> *The Beatles, 'Hey Jude' (1968)*

Niqnaaqpaadiwaaq (2012)
• Aqlaam • Aswaaq (Peintre Celebre)
Won just the one race, in 2015, from 25 tries.
> This old man, he played one,
> He played knick knack on my thumb.
> With a knick knack, paddy whack,
> Give a dog a bone.
> This old man came rolling home.

MONKHOUSE (2010)
• Scorpion • Gold Shot (Polish Precedent)

Comedian, scriptwriter, actor, chat and game show host, Bob Monkhouse (1928–2003) was very talented and had an amazing life but came across as smarmy. Maybe he wasn't. There doesn't seem to have been a racehorse named Bob Monkhouse but there's one called Monkhouse, so that will have to do because he wrote some wonderful gags and I want to include two of my favourites.

> They laughed when I said I was going to be a comedian. Well, they're not laughing now.

> I want to die peacefully in my sleep, like my father. Not screaming and terrified like his passengers.

Races won: He won a bumper race at Bangor in 2015.

Quite a good name

Chilblains (1978)
* *Hotfoot* • *Chiltern Red (Port Corsair)*
They didn't stop her winning a couple of races as a two-year-old before she emigrated to Italy, possibly to have them treated.

BROUGH SCOTT (1979)
* Steel Heart • Parthian Song (Parthia)

Writer, broadcaster, man of many parts, Brough Scott boasts the rare distinction of having both ridden as a jockey and been ridden by one. Born in 1942 and again in 1979, Brough Scott rode over 100 winners and has won many awards, including an MBE. As a horse, he received fewer accolades, although at Lingfield on 7 October 1982, ridden by Brian Rouse, Brough Scott won the 25-runner Dryhill Handicap at 33-1. It was a price his previous efforts fully justified.

In 1980 Scott had received a letter from a Mr Sullivan politely asking permission to name a yearling after him. 'I thought it rather pompous to refuse,' says Scott, 'and thought no more about it until the following summer when people teased me that my owner's business was pornography and he named his horses accordingly. The polite Mr Sullivan was David Sullivan, busy making a fortune from adult magazines. It was a relief when the horse was packed off to the Far East and his name changed!'

> And there's the unmistakable figure of Joe Mercer ...
> or is it Lester Piggott?
> *Brough Scott, commentating in 1981*

Races won: as a horse, just the one.

Fireplace (1978)

*   *Thatch* • *Gaia (Charlottesville)*

Fancy calling your pride and joy Fireplace. Undeterred, she was stoked up enough to win a maiden race at Fairyhouse in 1980.

Steelworks (1978)

*   *Steel Heart* • *Hariota (Hook Money)*

Fancy calling your pride and joy Steelworks. Rising above his name, he won six times between 1981 and 1983.

A jolly good name

Food Fight (1985)

*   Banquet Table • Violent Act (Vitriolic)

Won 20 times in the USA. They were only small races but if he'd been trained by Arthur Stephenson (who won the 1987 Cheltenham Gold Cup with The Thinker), he'd have said, 'Little fish are sweet,' because that's what Stephenson used to say.

CHARLIE GEORGE (1970)

*   Don Carlos • Courtsay (Sayajirao)

In 1971 Charlie George was transferred for 2,500 guineas. It was incredibly cheap for a player who, a few months earlier, had scored the winning goal in Arsenal's FA Cup Final victory over Liverpool, in front of a crowd of 100,000 at Wembley.

It was the second half of extra time. John Radford passed to Charlie George, the hero of the terraces, and from the edge of the penalty area George fired the ball into the left-hand corner of the net. Famously, he lay flat on his back, arms outstretched, and waited for teammates to haul him up. That sort of thing was a novelty then.

A boyhood Arsenal fan himself, George mixed with the fans and disdained both celebrity and authority. While today's stars pay a lot to have their hair styled exotically, George just let his grow. An argumentative rebel at a time when managers were often dictators, George said, 'If there was one thing I couldn't stand, it was being told what to do.' That was unfortunate, as Bertie Mee, Arsenal's manager, was a great believer in telling players what to do.

At his flashing best, Charlie George glided through defences like mercury, a magical presence. Then he became a horse and went to live in Peter Robinson's Newmarket yard.

He was owned by Jack Fisher, an Arsenal fan who had previously owned the useful David Jack and later the prolific winner Brady. Brady was named after Liam Brady, like David Jack an Arsenal star, not after Ian Brady, the Moors Murderer, or Tom Brady, the New England Patriots quarterback.

Fisher lived to be 100, dying in 2017. Charlie George, the horse, didn't last as long. Transferred for 2,900 guineas as a three-year-old, he was sold again for just 800 guineas as a four-year-old. He probably kicked against authority without the redeeming feature of being as quick as the Arsenal legend.

> Jumped over the fence into an Arsenal kit
> Scoring the best goals ever hit.
> Singing the Charlie George calypso
> Charlie George calypso
> Charlie George calypso
> Ipso facto he's number one.
> *Steven North and the Flat Back Four, 'The Charlie George Calypso'*

> I love my racing. I love a drink now and again and I enjoy doing nothing, just meeting and talking with friends.
> *Charlie George, 2005*

Races won: one each year in 1972, 1973 and 1974.

Dearie me

Bad Dog (2015)
• *Pastoral Pursuits* • *Movie Star (Barathea)*
What sort of a name is that for a horse? Couldn't he at least have been called Lassie?

CLAUDIO NICOLAI (1973)
• Diatome • Capriccioli (Saint Crespin III)

It was ironic that Claudio Nicolai was a baritone because something very similar – Baronet – was his downfall, and mine.

Born in Germany in 1929, Claudio Nicolai spent his life singing, mainly for the Cologne Opera. He sang and sang and in the 1970s combined singing with racing and gave that a good shot, too. Then the 1978 Cambridgeshire Handicap arrived.

The important thing about the 1978 race, in my opinion, was that I backed Claudio Nicolai at 33-1. He started at 10-1 and all went swimmingly until jockey Joe Mercer and Claudio Nicolai got boxed in inside the final furlong. When a gap finally came, it was too late. The next day the headline in the *Sporting Life* read, 'Claudio Nicolai is unlucky as Baronet lasts home.'

I suppose it's time to forgive and forget. Bum.

> Don Alfonso is played by baritone Claudio Nicolai and he's much lighter voiced than is usual for the role. This fits with an interpretation that is nuanced rather than buffo.
> *Review of a performance of* Cosi Fan Tutte *in Paris in 1992. Personally, I wouldn't know.*

Races won: four, including the 1976 William Hill Gold Cup at Redcar.

DOLLY PARTON (2008)
* Tagula * Batool (Bahri)

Dolly Parton has an enormously
successful career behind her and an
often remarked-upon front in front
of her. Dolly Parton the racehorse
also has a career behind her.

Born into dire poverty
in Tennessee in 1946, talent,
determination and force of
personality eventually converted
Dolly Parton into one of the biggest
selling, enduring and award-winning songwriters and singers of
modern times. She wrote and performed huge hits such as 'Coat
of Many Colours', 'Jolene' and 'I Will Always Love You'.

A country music star, she also showed herself to be an astute
businesswoman and generous philanthropist, her charitable work
focused on improving literacy.

Dolly Parton's equine namesake didn't quite match those
achievements, although we've yet to hear her sing. Two of Dolly
Parton's three wins, in 2010 and 2011, were in selling races. No one
bid for her, and in her final five outings Dolly Parton beat only two
of 49 opponents. No wonder she gave up after that.

> I was the first woman to burn my bra. It took
> the fire department four days to put it out.
> *Dolly Parton*

A dolly good name

Dolly Smarten (1982)
* *Smarten* * *La Cleavage (The Axe II)*
I'm pretty sure that Dolly Parton would approve of Harry 'Chips'
Landry's choice of name, even though Dolly Smarten only won

three small races at Finger Lakes and Rockingham Park in 1986 and 1987.

EARTHA KITT (2014)
• Pivotal • Ceiling Kitty (Red Clubs)

Bred and owned by Andrew Black's Chasemore Farm, Eartha Kitt's dam was Ceiling Kitty, which may help to explain the name. Perhaps Black, one of Betfair's founders, is a fan of the sultry singer and actress.

Eartha Kitt (1927–2008) was a one-off performer with a famously purry voice and sensual stage presence but her life was even more remarkable than her career. Born into poverty with the added burden of a black mother and unknown white father, rejected and uncared for, Kitt carried the pain of her childhood all her life but became a huge artistic success. Orson Welles described her as 'the most exciting woman in the world'.

In 1968, when she spoke out against the Vietnam War, she was ostracised and moved to France. She spoke four languages and sang in 11. She was a remarkable woman, a campaigner as well as a cabaret star.

> You send the best of this country off to be shot and maimed. No wonder the kids rebel and take pot.
> *Eartha Kitt to Lady Bird Johnson, wife of President Lyndon Johnson, at a White House dinner in 1968. It didn't go down well.*

Races won: three races in 2016 and 2017, including a Listed race.

Good and not so good

Hall Of Mirrors (1986)
• *Clever Trick* • *Reflection (Mill Reef)*
Owned by the Queen, won three small races in 1988 and 1989.

Hall Of Mirrors (2010)
• *Duke of Marmalade* • *Apache Dream (Indian Ridge)*
Bred in Ireland, won twice including a Group 3 race at the Curragh
in 2014. Later raced in Qatar.

FATS WALLER (1972)
• Sing Sing • Ragirl (Ragusa)

It's a great name, isn't it? It makes
you want to see him perform
although, as Fats died in 1943, he's not
giving live performances any more.
Captain John Macdonald-
Buchanan must have liked him
because the owner-breeder named
him. The Captain's own name was
the result of a mating between
Major Sir Reginald Macdonald
and Catherine Buchanan, of Buchanan's Black & White whisky
fame. They decided to become the Macdonald-Buchanans. Luckily,
when their son married Lady Rose Fane, the couple didn't agree to
become the Macdonald-Buchanan-Fanes, or where would it end?

Macdonald-Buchanan (1925–2014) proved himself a brave as
well as young tank commander in the Second World War, for
which he was awarded the Military Cross. I don't suppose you're
interested but in case you are Macdonald-Buchanan later ran
the Lavington Stud and filled several important posts in racing,
including that of Senior Steward of the Jockey Club.

Fats Waller, equine division, was slimmer and fitter than his namesake, and a good sprinter as a two-year-old before flagging as a three-year-old. As a four-year-old he failed to turn up at all.

No one to talk with, all by myself
No one to walk with, but I'm happy on the shelf
Ain't misbehavin', I'm savin' my love for you.
Fats Waller, 'Ain't Misbehavin'' (1929)

Races won: two in 1974.

GRONKOWSKI (2015)
• Lonrho • Four Sugars (Lookin At Lucky)

A lot of NFL players are very big; Rob Gronkowski is bigger. On the long list of things you don't want to experience in life, standing alone between 'Gronk' and your own team's end zone ranks highly.

You could try to tackle him around his ankles, you could try to wrap him in a warm embrace, or you could do the sensible thing and feign a heart attack. All options are likely to result in your humiliation and his latest touchdown. While he is celebrating you will be trying to stand up. As Gronkowski has almost three million followers on Twitter, you may get a mention there.

Gronkowski, the New England Patriots' star attacking tight end, is over six foot five inches tall with contents weighing about 19 stone. The equine version of Gronkowski is also big and strong and might conceivably be able to stop him, if eligible to play.

Illustrating the vagaries of the sales ring, Gronkowski was sold for $75,000 as a foal, for 50,000 guineas as a yearling and for 300,000 guineas as a two-year-old. It's nothing compared to the price the NFL player can command.

I love the New England Patriots and as Rob Gronkowski
is 6ft 5 inches and about the same wide, I thought it would

be an appropriate name for the horse, as he's built much
the same.
Kerri Radcliffe of owner Phoenix Thoroughbreds, 2018

Races won: four in a row, the fourth a Listed race at Newcastle.
The ambitious plan was to send him to the 2018 Kentucky Derby
but he caught a fever and was excused. Then his owners moved
him to America where he was runner-up in the Belmont Stakes.

A love name

Secret Romance (1977)
• *Clandestine* • *Sunny Fling (Ribot's Fling)*
There have been better Secret Romances, but none with a better
founded name. Between 1980 and 1984 Secret Romance won three
of his 56 races, at increasingly obscure racetracks, amassing career
earnings of less than $25,000. After winning twice at Suffolk Downs,
he won a race at the annual charity meeting at Ligonier, Pennsylvania,
in 1983 – the last year the meeting was held.

HITMAN HEARNS (2009)
• Milan • Desirable Asset (Zagreb)

If the horse had packed the same punch as Thomas 'The Hitman'
Hearns he'd have seen off every opponent. Sadly, he possessed
a light jab rather than a devastating hook.

In the 1980s, together with Sugar Ray Leonard, Marvin Hagler
and Roberto Duran, Hearns was involved in what aficionados
regard as some of the greatest fights with some of the greatest
fighters of all time.

A ferociously hard puncher, 48 of whose 61 wins were by
knockout, Hearns won world titles at five different weights. When
he fought Leonard in a unifying bout for the World Welterweight
title, in 1981, Hearns was unbeaten in 32 fights while Leonard

had lost once in 31. Ahead on points on all the judges' scorecards at the end of the thirteenth round, Hearns was stopped in the fourteenth. The pain of defeat was eased by a payout of about $8 million (about $21 million or £15 million today). Leonard ended up with about $11 million ($29 million or £21 million).

In 1984, Hearns beat Duran but the following year lost to 'Marvelous' Marvin Hagler. He had a good excuse: he broke his right hand in the first round.

> Some people are going to be happy [with my decision].
> Some people aren't. But I must live my life.
> *Thomas Hearns in 2005 on his decision to fight again, aged 46, after a five-year break. He won the bout, and won again on his final appearance the following year.*

Races won: having won a point-to-point in Ireland in 2014, Hitman Hearns won a hurdle race at Catterick in 2016.

HITMAN FRED (2013)
• Getaway • Garravagh Lass (Oscar)

Named after Colm 'Fast Fred' Hearne, an owner with Irish trainer Denis Paul Murphy, Hitman Fred wasn't in the same ring as Hitman Hearns.

Even so, having been bought by Bernice Murphy for €20,000 in June 2016, Hitman Fred won on his only point-to-point appearance in May 2017 and was sold ten days later for £90,000. Not bad. Now with trainer Rose Dobbin, he still has time to develop a knockout punch, or at least a jab.

HUMPHREY BOGART (2013)
• Tagula • Hazarama (Kahyasi)

Those wonderful films with Humphrey Bogart (1899–1957) playing the cynical hero – *The Maltese Falcon* (1941), *Casablanca* (1942), *The*

Big Sleep (1946) and *The African Queen* (1951) among them. They are enduring cinema classics, with Bogart himself unforgettable. That's if you've seen the films.

As a horse, Humphrey Bogart was less memorable but didn't disgrace his heritage and performed the useful role of reminding us of the original version. Well done.

> Of all the gin joints in all the towns in all the world, she walked into mine.
> *Rick Blaine (Humphrey Bogart) after his ex, the now-married Ilsa (Ingrid Bergman), enters his club.* Casablanca *(1942).*

Races won: three so far, including the 2016 Listed Lingfield Derby Trial. Humphrey Bogart finished fifth in the Derby. Now he's hurdling and won at Huntingdon in 2018.

INGLEBY MACKENZIE (2014)
• Sixties Icon • Natalie Jay (Ballacashtal)

Bred and initially owned and trained by a swashbuckling Hampshire footballer, Mick Channon, Ingleby Mackenzie was named after a swashbuckling Hampshire cricketer, Colin Ingleby-Mackenzie (1933–2006).

Both men were talented sportsmen and entertainers and both had a passion for horseracing. In Ingleby-Mackenzie's case, gambling featured prominently in his passion. At Eton the headmaster, Claude Elliott, lectured him on the evils of gambling. The lecture didn't work. In 1958, aged 24, Ingleby-Mackenzie became Hampshire's last amateur captain. His priorities were divided. As he explained in his autobiography, *Many A Slip* (1962), 'Our first championship match did not start until 10 May and I was therefore able to attend the Guineas meeting with a clear conscience.' Interviewed that year on BBC Television's *Junior Sportsview*, Ingleby-Mackenzie was asked the reason for Hampshire's success. 'Oh, wine, women and song,' he replied.

Interviewer: 'But don't you have certain rules, discipline, helpful hints for the younger viewer?'

Ingleby-Mackenzie: 'Well, everyone in bed in time for breakfast, I suppose.'

Despite or perhaps because of the captain's cavalier approach to the game, involving a lot of champagne, laughter and risky declarations, in 1961 Ingleby-Mackenzie led 'Happy Hants' to their first championship.

Racing was never forgotten. Hampshire bowler Malcolm Heath recalled, 'We never really felt he was 100 per cent with us after two o'clock.' On one occasion Ingleby-Mackenzie persuaded umpire Harry Baldwin to bring a radio onto the field so that he could hear an important race.

When Royal Ascot arrived, Ingleby-Mackenzie was prone to be ill, a medical condition repeated during Glorious Goodwood. Later, he was the proud part-owner of a Royal Ascot winner, when Camden Town won the 1978 Jersey Stakes.

> **EW 'Jim' Swanton:** 'I want you all to be in bed by 11.00.'
> **Colin Ingleby-Mackenzie:** 'I don't see how we can be in bed at 11.00 when we're due out on the field at 11.30.'
> *Colin Ingleby-Mackenzie when captain of EW Swanton's XI before a match in Trinidad, 1961.*

> Golf is a game to be played between cricket and death.
> *Colin Ingleby-Mackenzie*

Races won: The horse lacks the flair of the cricketer, but has won two races so far.

JACK HOBBS (2012)
• Halling • Swain's Gold (Swain)

It's all very well admiring Jack Hobbs (1882–1963) for his cricketing skills and personal qualities, but the fact that 'the Master' scored an enormous number of runs, played for England in 61 Test matches and was a hero of the 1920s doesn't alter the fact that his tally of centuries was 199 (or some say 197) and not 200. To me it seems a bit sloppy and lacking in perseverance.

In those days, even top-class professional sportsmen weren't paid huge sums and after a benefit season in 1919, Hobbs, who was from a poor background, bought a shop at 59 Fleet Street and opened Jack Hobbs Ltd, sports outfitters. He worked in the shop himself, particularly after retiring from cricket in 1934. He was knighted in 1953, although not for his work in the shop.

A fine batsman and an excellent racehorse.

> There is only one Master: Jack Hobbs.
> *Matthew Engel in The Essential Wisden: An Anthology*
> *of 150 Years of Wisden Cricketers' Almanack (2003)*

Races won: five between 2014 and 2017, notably the 2015 Irish Derby and 2017 Dubai Sheema Classic. Jack Hobbs also finished second in the 2015 Derby.

MAX MILLER (1988)
• Funny Man • Sizzle (High Line)

Max Miller's humour seems outdated now, but then so is Max Miller, who died in 1963.

'The Cheeky Chappie' was one of the most popular stand-up comedians of all time, in his comic prime in the 1940s and 1950s. As he told his music hall audiences, 'There'll never be another.' Armed with catchphrases – 'Now there's a funny thing' – and colourful clothing, Max Miller used innuendo and double entendre to skirt around the strict censorship in force at the time.

Not all his jokes were sexual. 'A Yorkshireman came to London and he couldn't get any Yorkshire pudding, so he went home and battered himself to death.' Other jokes came close to getting Miller banned, although he never was. High on the list was his story of the time: 'I was walking along this narrow mountain pass, so narrow that nobody else could pass you, when I saw a beautiful blonde walking towards me. A beautiful blonde with not a stitch on. I didn't know whether to toss myself off or block her passage.'

Max Miller was much more successful as a comedian than a racehorse. Reborn, the well-named Max Miller only ran twice and not very fast.

> **Man**: 'I like seeing experienced girls home.'
> **Girl**: 'But I'm not experienced.'
> **Man**: 'You're not home yet.'
> *Max Miller, c. 1950*

MICKEY PEARCE (2002)
* Rossini * Lucky Coin (Hadeer)

For 20 years, off and on, Mickey Pearce was in and out of the Nag's Head pub, wearing his trademark trilby and telling Del Boy and Rodney about his latest imaginary entrepreneurial success. A regular in *Only Fools and Horses* between 1983 and 2003, actor Patrick Murray subsequently had a colourful life, sometimes in Spain, sometimes in Thailand, sometimes in the Gardeners Arms pub in Higham in Kent. He has had all sorts of jobs, including as a professional poker player, DJ and taxi driver, so the transition to being a horse came relatively easily.

Mickey Pearce wasn't a great horse but he did win five times in 2006 and 2007, all selling hurdles, and he had one significant claim to fame. At Hereford on 20 March 2006, Mickey Pearce beat a horse called The Wife's Sister. Nearing the finish the pair collided, prompting a stewards' inquiry. The stewards' report

stated, 'They found that the winner, Mickey Pearce, ridden by
S. Crawford, had interfered with The Wife's Sister.' Despite this
rather serious finding, the result was allowed to stand, although
Crawford was suspended for four days. Doubtless he was also
warned against his future behaviour.

> See the blonde bird? I've had her! And her mate. See that
> black sort at the back there? She's crazy about me! Phones
> me all the time.
> *Mickey Pearce, 'Yuppy Love' episode,* Only Fools and Horses
> *(1989)*

NICK THE BRIEF (1982)
* Duky • Roman Twilight (Romulus)

John Upson was a civil engineer who employed the services of
barrister Nicholas Wilson. In 1985 Upson bought a three-year-
old for IR9,000 guineas and named it Nick The Brief in Wilson's
honour. Both went on to great things. In 1987 Wilson became a QC
and in the same year Nick The Brief made his debut. By the end of
the year he had won two hurdle races.

A stout galloper, favoured by soft ground, Nick The Brief's
proudest moments came when, trained by Upson, he won the 1990
Peter Marsh Chase and Irish Gold Cup Chase, and in 1991 the Irish
version of the Hennessy Cognac Gold Cup. The latter two races
were one and the same, with different names.

Wilson did even better and in 2011 became a Justice of the
Supreme Court of the UK, assuming the title of Lord Wilson
of Culworth.

> I thought he was a penalty kick that day. In soft ground
> he was top class – he would gallop them into submission.
> *John Upson looking back on Nick The Brief's victory in the
> 1991 Irish Hennessy Cognac Gold Cup*

You will say, 'Well, at the very minimum, marriage can take place only between two living persons.' Actually, not so! Apparently about 20 posthumous marriages take place every year in France. You have to prove that you were genuinely engaged to the deceased and that his/her parents still approve of the marriage.
Lord Wilson of Culworth, in an address at Queen's University, Belfast, February 2014

Races won: 11 in all but the ones I've mentioned are the ones that matter most.

Legal names

Chutzpah (1992)
• Minshaanshu Amad • Tressa (Parisianne)
An excuse for giving a lawyer's definition of chutzpah, a Yiddish word meaning audacity or cheek.
    A child is convicted of murdering both his parents. He pleads with the judge for mercy, on the grounds that he is an orphan.
Races won: three in Illinois in 1994 and 1995.

Recuse (1992)
• Skip Trial • Goholm (Noholme II)
Won seven small races at Suffolk Downs and Rockingham between 1994 and 1998.

PERCY THROWER (1987)
• Oats • Arctic Advert (Birdbrook)

---

and

PERCY THROWER (2014)
• Sir Percy • Dayrose (Daylami)

Percy Thrower knew his onions, although he knew his roses better, and when it came to parsnips, he preferred to hand over to Arthur Billitt. In the early 1970s, Billitt was Thrower's co-presenter on *Gardeners' World* but it was Percy Thrower who became the face and name of gardening. For over 30 years he was the gardening guru on a succession of radio and television programmes. Percy Thrower was to gardening what Barry Bucknell was to do-it-yourself. It's not my fault if you're too young to have watched *Barry Bucknell's Do It Yourself* programme.

Mary Hambro must have liked Percy Thrower because she named the 1987 one, although the 2014 one had a more 'Percy Thrower' pedigree. So far, it hasn't done him any good. I expect there'll be a Monty Don soon.

Nothing much wrong with that, is there, Arthur?
Percy Thrower's catchphrase on Gardeners' World.

She's seen more beds than Percy Thrower's trowel.
An expression of the time

Races won: 1987 version, four between 1994 and 1996. 2014 version, none so far.

A horticultural celebrity

Rose To Fame (2014)
• Fame and Glory • Cinderella Rose (Midnight Legend)
Barely broken the surface yet but hopefully will blossom in time.

FORK HANDLES (2008)
* Doyen * Natalie Jay (Ballacashtal)

Bred, trained and initially owned by Mick Channon, who must like the celebrated sketch from *The Two Ronnies*. Broadcast in 1976, it takes place in Ronnie Corbett's hardware shop. The joke revolves around a misunderstanding; Ronnie Barker asks for fork 'andles and Corbett offers him four candles.

It seemed funny at the time and admirers of the sketch can reminisce in the Four Candles pub in Oxford. While there they might like to recall the two races Fork Handles won in 2010 and 2012.

PETE AND DUD (1979)
* Owen Dudley * Athena Royale (Athens Wood)

Peter Cook and Dudley Moore were icons of satirical comedy in the 1960s and 1970s, graduating from the revue *Beyond the Fringe*, which also starred Alan Bennett and Jonathan Miller, to the groundbreaking television success, *Not Only... But Also*.

The latter featured Pete and Dud as working-class characters wearing mackintoshes and flat caps, discussing social and political issues with confident ignorance.

Cook was an inspirational, innovative comic, regarded as the more creative talent, but it was Moore whose career blossomed when he moved to Hollywood and starred in *10* (1979) and *Arthur* (1981). Their stories were both comic and sad. Moore's success coupled with Cook's heavy drinking took its toll on their relationship.

In later life Cook (1937–1995), a major supporter of *Private Eye*, often appeared on chat shows, rarely wholly sober but invariably amusing. Moore's final years were marred by a rare brain disease, from which he died in 2002, aged 66.

It's a good excuse for a few gems.

I met a man at a party. He said, 'I'm writing a novel.'
I said, 'Oh, really? Neither am I.'
Peter Cook

I'd rather have been a judge than a miner. Being a miner, as
soon as you are too old and tired and sick and stupid to do
the job properly, you have to go. The very opposite applies
with judges.
Peter Cook

Peter Cook: 'You rang?'
David Frost: 'Peter, I'm having a little dinner party on
behalf of Prince Andrew and Sarah Ferguson. I know
they'd love to meet you, big fans. It'd be super if you could
make it – Wednesday the 12th.'
Peter Cook: 'Hang on, I'll just check my diary. Oh dear,
I find I'm watching television that night.'

Alan Bennett recalled that the only regret Cook ever voiced
was that he'd saved Frost from drowning in 1963.

I'm always looking for meaningful one-night stands.
Dudley Moore

Races won: you needed a sense of humour to own Pete And Dud
because he was a dud, recording a score of 0 from 26 on the Flat
and over jumps between 1981 and 1987.

A marriage name

Wedding Picture (1981)
• Blushing Groom • Strike A Pose (Iron Ruler)
Not only got in the frame but won six of her first seven starts, including
the Pinafore Stakes at Suffolk Downs in 1984. Went on to win twice

more in 1985, including the Listed Revidere Handicap at Saratoga, from only 14 career starts. One of the more successful marriages.

PETER O'TOOLE (1975)
* Streetfighter * Good Oil (Darling Boy)

Peter O'Toole's father was a racecourse bookmaker, so there were horses in the family, but O'Toole proved hopeless as a racehorse, failing to reach the winning post first in 11 undistinguished appearances from 1977 to 1979.

O'Toole's strengths lay elsewhere, on the stage and film set. His film career took off after starring in *Lawrence of Arabia* in 1962 and he was nominated for the Academy Award for Best Actor eight times, without ever winning it.

Never mind, the performance that mattered most was as Jeffrey Bernard in *Jeffrey Bernard is Unwell*, which opened at the Apollo Theatre in Shaftesbury Avenue in 1989 and ran for a year, with successful revivals.

Bernard wrote a memorable column for *The Sporting Life* from 1970 to 1971, when he was sacked. From 1978 he reached a wider audience with his 'Low Life' column in *The Spectator*. The play's title was based on the note which appeared in *The Spectator* when Bernard's column was absent through alcohol, although *The Sporting Life* could claim to have got there first. It periodically reported, 'Jeffrey Bernard is ill. It is hoped that his column will be resumed shortly.'

Bernard, played magnificently by Peter O'Toole, gets locked in the Coach and Horses pub in Soho – Bernard's main home – for the night, with his reminiscences, a bottle of vodka, and a collection of ghosts from the past. It was very funny, although scratching at the line between comedy and tragedy. If only the racehorse had been as entertaining.

When the doorbell rang this morning, I was sure it
was the Grim Reaper, but luckily it was the milkman.
*Jeffrey Bernard's words while ill in 1982, spoken by Peter
O'Toole seven years later.*

Races won: nil.

JOG (1977)
• Mount Hagen • Strolling Sweetly (Le Levanstall)

Not really a fast enough pace for horseracing but did win a hurdle
race at Tramore. He's here as an excuse for another Jeffrey Bernard
anecdote. Bernard had been admitted to hospital. The doctor was
studying his notes.

> **Doctor:** 'You drink and smoke a horrendous amount.
> Why do you drink?'
> **Jeffrey Bernard:** 'To stop me jogging.'
> *Jeffrey Bernard's 'Low Life' column in* The Spectator,
> *22 October 1983*

WG GRACE (2015)
• Exceed And Excel • Ownwan (Kingmambo)

WG Grace – he probably didn't have any names, just initials –
was famous for his beard (impressive) and his pioneering cricketing
skills (ditto).

Grace (1848–1915) dominated cricket throughout his adult life,
even when his body became twice as large as when he first played
the game. He excelled at batting, bowling, fielding, captaincy and
longevity, playing for 44 seasons.

His equine namesake is unlikely to last that long, as the average
lifespan of thoroughbreds is between 25 and 30 years.

They came to see me bat, not you umpire.
WG Grace carrying on after being given out LBW. An
alternative version has Grace saying the same to the bowler
while replacing the bails after being bowled first ball.

Races won: so far, one. WG Grace would not have been impressed.

An eye-catching name

Rhett Butler (1970)
• Bold Lad • Pussy Galore (High Hat)
Clark Gable played Rhett Butler in the 1939 film version of Margaret
Mitchell's 1936 novel *Gone with the Wind*. Curiously, the equine Rhett
Butler was a gelding and scored only once, in a maiden race at
Newcastle in 1974.

Good show

Libby T Valance (2011)
• Scorpion • Dipp In The Dark (Presenting)
Maybe it's not that clever but I like it. *Liberty Valance*, the baddie in the
classic Western *The Man Who Shot Liberty Valance*, was not available.
Not only was he dead but his name had already been taken. The 1962
film, directed by John Ford, brought together James Stewart, John
Wayne and Lee Marvin. Marvin was the baddie, Stewart, alias Ranse
Stoddard, the man who stood up to him and Wayne, alias Tom
Doniphon, the man who ... you'd better see it.

When the legend becomes fact, print the legend.
Maxwell Scott (played by Carleton Young), a reporter.

Nothing's too good for the man who shot Liberty Valance.
Jason Tully (played by Willis Bouchey), a train conductor, The Man
Who Shot Liberty Valance *(1962)*

Races won: Libby T Valance won a bumper race in 2016. Liberty Valance won a maiden race on the Flat in 2008.

A fine name

Custard The Dragon (2013)
• Kyllachy • Autumn Pearl (Orpen)
I just like it. Named after Ogden Nash's 1936 poem about the dragon who was a coward but saved the day by swallowing a pirate.

> Custard the dragon had big sharp teeth,
> And spikes on top of him and scales underneath,
> Mouth like a fireplace, chimney for a nose,
> And realio, trulio, daggers on his toes.

Races won: Custard The Dragon won seven races on the Flat between 2016 and 2018, so far.

A grand name

That's Your Lot (1982)
• Auction Ring • Guillotina (Busted)
An excellent name and not a bad horse, winning three times on the Flat and twice over hurdles.

Queer Street (1970)
• Busted • County Court (Grey Sovereign)
From the days when 'queer' wasn't invariably used to mean homosexual and when 'Queer Street' was regularly used to mean broke.

Sadly, Queer Street may have helped put Queer Street's owner in Queer Street as, in eight outings, she failed to reach a place.

'You see, I've run rather short.'

'Yes?' said my father without any sound of interest.

'In fact I don't quite know how I'm going to get through the next two months.'

'Well, I'm the worst person to come to for advice. I've never been "short" as you so painfully call it. And yet what else could you say? Hard up? Penurious? Distressed? Embarrassed? Stony-broke? On the rocks? In Queer Street? Let us say you are in Queer Street and leave it at that.'

Evelyn Waugh, Brideshead Revisited *(1945). Charles Ryder appraises his father Edward of his financial problems.*

8. BARRED NAMES

This section is very short to make you feel that you are getting through the book quicker.

You can't give a racehorse any name (see the section headed 'Weatherbys – The Nexus of Names'). No name must contain more than 18 characters, including signs and spaces. Numbers aren't allowed. Nor are all sorts of other things (ditto).

For good or ill, by the time the authorities close the stable door some horses have already bolted, galloping their suggestive names around international racecourses.

It was always thus. The 1815 St Leger was won by Filho da Puta, owned by Sir William Maxwell. *Filho da puta* is Portuguese for 'son of a whore' and despite having fewer than 18 characters would nowadays be unlikely to be allowed into Doncaster racecourse.

Maxwell had a good excuse for his equine outburst, having lost an arm at the Battle of Corunna in Spain in 1809. Luckily it was his left arm.

In 1930, perhaps inspired by Sir William's example, Lord Rosebery won the Yorkshire Cup with The Bastard, who went on to finish third in the Ascot Gold Cup before being exported to Australia as a stallion.

His new owner, Jack McDougall, considered his acquisition's name unseemly, and changed it to The Buzzard. It worked because The Buzzard was champion sire in Australia in 1946/47 and 1949/50 and his many successful offspring included two winners of the Melbourne Cup, Rainbird and Old Rowley.

A name innocuous in one era may be less so in another. Modern eyebrows might rise at the winner of the 1834 Oaks – Pussy.

Perhaps the worst Oaks upon record.
*George Tattersall's verdict on Pussy's 1834 Classic success,
in* The Cracks of the Day *(1840).*

A bum name

Superbum (1970)

* *Super Sam* • *Bottoms Up (Preciptic)*

Even with a super bum the filly managed to win only once, a seller
at Brighton in 1973.

9. SEXCETERA

People responded with heartwarming enthusiasm to my request for clever racehorse names. There was particular enthusiasm for sex and vulgarity, sometimes both, with repeated relish for the likes of Mary Hinge, Muff Diver, Noble Locks and, of course, Big Tits. I like to think the suggestions were made with the intention of raising the tone of the book.

Several of the suggested names had failed to survive Weatherbys' scrutiny but Norfolk In Chance, Betty Swallocks, Penny Tration, Sofa King Fast and others live on in the suspect minds of some race fans, who clearly wish that Weatherbys' filter system had failed, as it sometimes had.

So here goes. It's not classy but I expect you'll enjoy it. Those liable to be appalled might like to skip this section, although I don't suppose they will.

SEXCETERA (1999)
• Roo Art • Chic Paree (High Street)

In 1998 Playboy TV launched *Sexcetera*, which ran until 2005. Perhaps Landon Burchell watched it, because in 1999 a foal bred and owned by his Burchell Farm Company in Texas was named after the programme.

Sexcetera wasn't much good as a racehorse, his sole success from 35 tries coming in a humble maiden claiming race at Lone Star Park in 2003, but he was noticed.

The sort of names to be prepared for

Sex Machine (1997)
* Shagny • Dominuette (Domino)
The sire may have something to do with it. Sex Machine won seven times in Australia before moving to California, where he won another five races.

Pleasure Me (1978)
* Pleasure Castle • Janie Kay (Lucky Oscar)
Raced briefly and unfulfullingly in Louisiana in 1980 and 1981.

Sheila Blige (1999)
* Zamindar • Stripanoora (Ahanoora)
Owned by Julie Mitchell, Sheila Blige won on her debut at Warwick in 2001 but in 2002 decided she wouldn't any more.

HOT PANTS (1969)
* Sea Hawk II • Minia (Sicambre)

When Royal Ascot made its annual appearance in 1971, hot pants were at the height of their popularity, although not with the crusty Duke of Norfolk, the Queen's representative.

In April, when it was rumoured that hot pants would be allowed into Ascot's hallowed enclosures, the Duke moved swiftly to crush such hopes. 'I wish to make it abundantly clear,' he declared, 'that the only form of ladies' trousers permitted will be suits with long trousers.'

So it was optimistic of porn star Linda Lovelace to turn up three years later in a silver Rolls-Royce bearing the number plate PEN15 while wearing a see-through blouse. A gentleman in a bowler hat refused to admit her, leaving Lovelace to pose for photographers on the bonnet of her car. The photographers seemed to enjoy it.

Several racehorses on several continents have been named Hot Pants, racing in Mexico and Australia, Canada and Brazil. Still, I'm sticking with the one that Doug Marks trained in Lambourn, even though he was a colt.

Those hot pants of hers were so damned tight, I could
hardly breathe.
Benny Hill

Races won: won twice at Cagnes-sur-Mer in 1972.

Priaprism (1986)
• *Full Out* • *Pleased Miss (What A Pleasure)*
The spelling amiss but the intention clear. Won six times at Suffolk
Downs, Penn National and Mountaineer between 1989 and 1991.

Martha Spanks (1980)
• *Home Guard* • *Amazer (Mincio)*
I can only tell you what I've read. The filly won once, in 1982, when
owned by Mrs R. Lamb.

PURE LUST (1979)
• Sallust • St Rosalie (Aureole)

A clever name and, given St Rosalie's lifestyle, lust unrequited.
Saint Rosalie, if she existed, was a hermit who lived in a cave on
a mountain overlooking Palermo in Sicily in the twelfth century.
Sallust was an Italian historian at the time of Julius Caesar with
a lifestyle that Saint Rosalie would not have approved of.

She was reputed to have been a big help when a plague struck
Palermo in 1624. Saint Rosalie guided a resident to the cave where
she had died. Her bones were then paraded around the city three
times and the plague ended. It's an unusual treatment for serious
illness but if you're at death's door it might be worth a try.

Palermo was impressed, making Saint Rosalie its patron saint.
So was Anthony Van Dyck (1599–1641), who painted *Saint Rosalie
Interceding for the Plague-Stricken of Palermo*. If you go to the

Metropolitan Museum of Art in New York, it's in Gallery 630.

I, Rosalia, daughter of Sinibald, Lord of Roses, and
Quisquina, have taken the resolution to live in this cave
for the love of my Lord, Jesus Christ.
*Saint Rosalie's inscription on her cave wall. Oh, well, it takes
all sorts.*

Races won: none.

CASSANOVA'S STORY (1978)
• Immortal Love • Havelotte (Haven)

There seems to be an extra 's'. Never mind: Giacomo Casanova
(1725–98) did everything to excess.

In his notorious *Histoire de ma Vie*, a 3,700-page autobiography
written between 1789 and 1798, Casanova chronicled over 120
affairs with countesses, nuns, milkmaids and every class of woman
in between. Yet although Casanova has long been a synonym for
a serial seducer, his life was more all-embracing than that all-
embracing aspect of it.

He was a writer and traveller who mixed with intellectuals and
scientists during the Age of Enlightenment and the *Histoire de ma Vie*
is now considered to be a valuable work of literature – erotic literature.

In 2010 an anonymous benefactor paid $9.6 million for the
original manuscript and donated it to the Bibliothèque Nationale
de France in Paris. The following year the Library staged an
exhibition, 'Casanova – The Passion of Freedom'.

The chief business of my life has always been to indulge my
senses; I never knew anything of greater importance. I felt
myself born for the fair sex, I have ever loved it dearly, and
I have been loved by it as often and as much as I could.
Giacomo Casanova, Histoire de ma Vie

We are particularly proud of presenting, for the first time ever, this great masterpiece of French literature. Casanova was a man who loved women, a charmer, not a predator who exploited them. He was always tender, never cruel. A feminist. *Bruno Racine, director of the Bibliothèque Nationale de France, 2011*

Races won: just one hurdle race in 1984. Too exhausted to win any more.

SIXTY NINE (1960)
* Greek Star * dam said to be Bannon Lass

---

and

SOIXANTE NEUF (1964)
* Coronation Year * Bewildered Anne (Bewildered)

Even in the Swinging Sixties sexual practices were generally less exotic than today and the linguistic knowledge of Weatherbys' staff less extensive.

In the 1960s, nightclub owner Joe Lisle had a club in Newcastle called Club 69. He brought Bunny Girls to his clubs and drove a Rolls-Royce with the registration JL 69. Lisle also had horses in training with Denys Smith and named two of them after Club 69.

Sixty Nine was a high-class chaser, winning 13 races between 1965 and 1971, including the 1967 Kirk and Kirk Chase and 1968 Great Yorkshire Chase.

Having got Sixty Nine into the public arena, Lisle quickly followed up with Soixante Neuf, who won six jumps races between 1967 and 1973.

It was a great club. Joe made his money but remained very down-to-earth, the money never changed him. One day two of his horses won and everyone in the club had backed

them. Champagne flowed like water.
Bob Blenkinsop, who married one of Club 69's Bunny Girls

Mary Hinge (1991)
* *Dowsing* • *Jeanne Avril (Music Boy)*

Mary Hinge was bought by trainer Julie Cecil as a yearling. The filly won five times, including a Listed race in 1994. Cecil must have been quite fond of her.

Muff Diver (1975)
* Deep Diver • Idiots Delight

An international performer, Muff Diver started his racing career in Ireland in 1977, then won several times in Belgium before joining trainer Bill Haigh in Yorkshire. By then he was exhausted and didn't win again.

HARLOT (2000)
* Bal Harbour • Queen Of The Quorn (Governor General)

In 2001 Harlot was bought at the Doncaster Sales for 1,000 guineas, cash. Despite her being a half-sister to Half A Knicker, trainer John Berry failed to score with her (sorry, it's a feeble joke, I just couldn't stop myself). After 11 goes, mainly at Lingfield, Harlot was retired in 2004.

If a woman hasn't got a tiny streak of harlot in her, she's a dry stick as a rule.
DH Lawrence, 1929

STRUMPETS

The splendidly named...

STRUMPET (1998)
* *Tragic Role* • *Fee (Mandamus)*

... was bred and initially owned by Lord and Lady Rothschild. Strumpet won a maiden fillies' race in 2000 and a selling race the following year. Age impaired her desirability. Bought for 10,000 guineas in 2000, a year later she was sold for 3,200 guineas.

Strumpet's mantle was taken up by *Storming Strumpet (2010)*, who won a bumper, a hurdle and a chase for trainer Tom George between 2014 and 2017.

> There's not a modest maiden elf
> But dreads the final Trumpet,
> Lest half of her should rise herself,
> And half some local strumpet!
> *Thomas Hardy, 'The Levelled Churchyard' (1882)*

More names

Trollop (1807)
* *Waxy* • *Trull (Volunteer)*
Trollop is a splendid name, on a par with Strumpet. Trull was a word for a prostitute.

Shy Talk (1976)
* *Sharpen Up* • *Skymistress (Skymaster)*
The dubiously named Shy Talk won twice for Neil Adam as a two-year-old in 1978 and twice again for Arthur Jones in 1981. Arthur was a lovely person. Just thought I'd say.

THE HAPPY HOOKER (1971)
 • Town Crier • Legal Love (King's Bench)

Rupert Deen was a member of the British team at the 1972 winter Olympic Games in Japan, competing in the luge. As Algy Cluff, a celebrated oil entrepreneur and former owner of *The Spectator*, observed at Deen's memorial service, the event was 'entirely suited to Rupert's requirements, since it is the only sport with the participant lying flat on his back'.

Deen (1938–2016) finished 43rd of 44 competitors in the men's singles but judging from a photograph of him and fellow team members in a pool, attended by Japanese women, he would have considered the Games a great success.

Deen's greatest achievement was to have Emanuel Emile Deen as his grandfather, resulting in an enormous inheritance which meant, as he told journalist Polly Toynbee when he was 41, 'I've always had everything I wanted, all my life.'

What he wanted above all was a riotous time full of women and champagne, in 'a luxurious bachelor life' that also found time for the major race meetings. In 1989, Taki, a Greek journalist best known for his 'High Life' column in *The Spectator*, noted admiringly that Deen was 'still wenching and boozing it up'. Despite his hedonistic lifestyle, the 'Old Harrovian seducer' managed to live to be 78, dying in St Tropez.

Deen was very familiar with hookers, and he picked a fine one when buying The Happy Hooker.

In 1971, Xaviera Hollander's book *The Happy Hooker* appeared. A $1,000-a-night call girl, Hollander set up a brothel in Manhattan called the Vertical Whorehouse. When it was closed down in 1971 Hollander left America and thrived on her frank memoirs.

In 1975 they were made into a film of the same name starring Lynn Redgrave as an unlikely call girl. Nowadays Hollander runs Xaviera's Happy Home bed-and-breakfast establishment in Amsterdam, where you can stay for £100 a night.

In the years of my youth, I counted among my friends
Charles Benson, Sir William Pigott-Brown, Rupert Deen,
Dai Llewellyn, Nigel Dempster and Lord Lucan. With the
exception of his lordship, what united us all was a love for
hookers and drink.
Taki, 'High Life', The Spectator, 28 October 1989

Races won: 11 between 1974 and 1977.

THE HAPPY HOOKER (2014)
* Dubleo * Lovey Amazon (Snaadee)

Less happy hooking in Australia, with three well-beaten runs so far.

Yet more names

Geespot (1999)
* *Pursuit Of Love* * *My Discovery (Imperial Frontier)*
There are rude names, risqué names and clever names. Geespot was
risqué and clever. Well done to Philip Bouchier-Hayes, a friend of trainer
Dominic Ffrench Davis, who suggested the name. The filly was not
a monotonous winner, but did win two selling races in 2002.

Buff Naked (2001)
* Pine Bluff * Demi Buff (Triocala)
Naked or not, Buff Naked won twice at Belmont in 2004.

POLLY ADLER (2007)
* Fantastic Light * Urania (Most Welcome)

Polly Adler wasn't a prostitute herself but for over 40 years supplied
others on a grand scale in New York, where she was known as 'the
Queen of Tarts'. Polly's was a high-class brothel, from 1924 based
at the Majestic at 215 West 75th Street. Elegantly furnished, the

Majestic attracted not only New York's mayor, Jimmy Walker, world heavyweight boxing champion Jack Dempsey and gangsters Dutch Schultz and Lucky Luciano but also writers Robert Benchley and Dorothy Parker, who gave advice on titles for the brothel's library. Years after the library closed, Adler's bestselling autobiography, *A House Is Not A Home* (1953), appeared.

Polly Adler was more successful as a madam than a racehorse, failing to win in nine attempts in 2011 and 2012. Her alter ego, *Queen Of The Tarts (2011) Royal Applause – Tart And A Half (Distant Relative),* fared no better, racing only as a two-year-old in 2013 when, in nine tries, she also failed to win. The only difference between women who marry to get their bills paid or to get away from disagreeable relatives and my girls is that my girls give a man his money's worth.

Polly Adler in A House Is Not A Home *(1953)*

Jafeica (1991)
• Dance Of Life • Moretta (Artaius)
I thought it was an obscene question but it turns out it was just an acronym
for Just Another Fucking Expense I Can't Afford. He wasn't a bad buy,
though. Jafeica cost 18,000 guineas and won three times in 1993 and 1994.

Finmental (1990)
• Nordance • Prima Bella (High Hat)
Bred in Ireland, Finmental raced only as a two-year-old, winning twice
for trainer Alan Bailey in 1992.

GIGOLOS

As in life, so in racing, gigolos are less common than strumpets. Yet
they've had their moments. *Gigolo (1945) Desmondtoi – Court Ballet
(Ballynahinch)* won the 1953 Tote Eider Chase and finished fourth
in the 1955 Grand National.

American Gigolo (2012) Azamour – Sadie Thompson (King's Best),
appropriately named given his dam (see section 6), won a bumper,
a hurdle and three Flat races between 2016 and 2018.

French Gigolo (2000) Pursuit of Love – French Mist (Mystiko) was less
successful, failing to score in ten attempts between 2002 and 2006.

The cleverly named *Lawn Lothario (1994) Pursuit of Love – Blade
Of Grass (Kris)* won four times in 1997 but the joy of success was
tempered by the fact that he had been gelded the previous year.

STUD MUFFIN (1992)
• Your Dancer • Creista (Truxton King)

Stud Muffin appeared in New Mexico and won a couple of small
races at Albuquerque and Santa Fé (great names – they make me
want to go there) in 1996 and 1997. A better one, *Stud Muffin (2004)*,
raced in New York from 2006 to 2012, winning 14 times and
earning over $670,000.

That's about it, really.

Black marks

Knobgobbler (1993)
* *Turkey Shoot* • *Pearly Mae (Best Of It)*
Whatever next? Won three from 26 between 1995 and 1997. Probably best forgotten.

Tihsho (1992)
* Homebuilder • Norene's Nemesis (King Emperor)
Someone at the American Jockey Club forgot to read the name backwards. Won eight small races between 1994 and 2000.

NOBLE LOCKS (1998)
* Night Shift • Imperial Graf (Blushing John)

A gelding, needless to say, Noble Locks was bred in Ireland but raced exclusively in Britain. Having been bought for 17,000 guineas as a yearling, he started out by finishing second in a selling race at Southwell in 2000. No sooner had Noble Locks not won than he was promptly claimed for £5,000 by trainer Kevin Ryan and equipped with Paul Dixon's colours.

Noble Locks won five times for Ryan and Dixon before being claimed for £6,000 by trainer James Unett, for whom he won three more races. I don't know what happened to him after that.

> There he is, with his noble locks, now as remarkable as when covered with snow, as when their dark honours curled around his manly face.
> Gentleman's Magazine, *1837. Obituary of the actor and theatre manager Jack Bannister (1760–1836). Reads like b******s to me.*

Races won: I've just told you. He won eight times from 2002 to 2003, all little ones at all-weather tracks.

> **HOOF HEARTED (1981)**
> • Docile Boy • Silver Sails (Jet Sail)

Merv Nelson, a breeder in British Columbia, blames his brother for the horse's name. Race callers had plenty of chances to work out the best way to deal with it because Hoof Hearted ran 65 times between 1983 and 1988, mainly at Exhibition Park, with rare outings to Sandown Park, Vancouver.

The filly won nine times, but they were all tiny races and her total earnings were only $40,000. Still, she made her mark in other ways, and she was not alone.

> **HOOF HEARTED (2000)**
> • Joshua Dancer • Zip Your Lip (Palace Music)

Bred and raced in South Africa, Hoof Hearted ran in at least ten maiden races in 2003 and 2004, but when Christmas arrived he still was one.

A name lacking in class

Passing Wind (1994)
• *Beau Zephyr* • *Miss Row (Long Row)*
Bred in New Zealand, he was remarkable only for his name. Passing Wind won once over hurdles in 2001 and once over fences in 2003, from 19 tries.

> **BIG TITS (2000)**
> • Lost World • Abigaila (River River)

Difficult not to spot but the Lellouche family, who bred, owned and trained Big Tits, managed to fool France Galop by the simple expedient of using English in France. Somehow Big Tits squeezed through. She was entitled to run in Britain but to the relief of the British Horseracing Board and the disappointment of journalists,

Big Tits was only displayed in France.

Having failed to be sufficiently prominent for trainer Elie Lellouche's liking in 2003, Big Tits moved to Jean-Pierre Girard, for whom she failed seven more times. Her final appearance was in an amateur riders' race at Granville-St-Pair-Sur-Mer in 2004, when ridden by Miss Isabelle Chipaux. I expect the crowd was vocal.

> We were having a family lunch and were trying to come up with ideas. My son suggested Gros Nichons, but that wouldn't have got past France Galop, so we decided on the English equivalent.
> *Elie Lellouche throws light on Big Tits*

Races won: none in 13 tries but attracted more attention than many much better racehorses.

There's no end to the names

Bad Girls Have Fun (2003)

• *Smart Strike* • *Lucky Chat (Lucky North)*

Not that much fun. Racing in Louisiana, Bad Girls Have Fun won just once from 36 tries. In 2008, as a five-year-old, she finally won a maiden race at Fair Grounds.

Lady Clitico (2011)

• *Bushranger* • *Villa Nova (Petardia)*

Maybe I'm mistaken. Evidently Clitico is a grammatical term. Anyway, she's won three times on the Flat in Ireland and England since 2013.

BODACIOUS TATAS (1985)
• *Distinctive Pro* • *Key To Paree (L'Enjoleur)*

So that's what it means. Caesar Kimmel at play again. Bodacious Tatas was trained by his son John and, racing mainly in New York and New Jersey, won 11 races and over $430,000 between 1987 and 1991.

Molly Pitcher has Bodacious Tatas.
Headline in local paper following Bodacious Tatas' success in the 1989 Molly Pitcher Handicap at Monmouth Park.

Names for wishful thinkers

She's Insatiable (2008)
* Ustinov • Checkered Past (Pentire)
Won six races in New Zealand in 2013 and 2014.

She Can't Say No (1989)
* Nasty and Bold • Sweet n Pretty Too (Drone)
Although she said no to racing. Having been sold in Texas for $3,200 in 1995 she was sold again, unraced, for $2,000 in 2000.

She's Easy (1978)
* T.V. Doubletalk • Shaggy Girl (Potomac)
Won eight times between 1982 and 1984, seven at Turf Paradise in Arizona and once at Les Bois Park in Idaho. They were bottom-of-the-ladder events. She's Easy's career earnings were less than $19,000.

MICHAEL BELL AND HAYLEY TURNER

Trainer Michael Bell played a big part in guiding Hayley Turner towards the top rank of jockeys. By coincidence, they found themselves training and riding horses which invited banter.

TURN ME ON (2003)
* Tagula • Jacobina (Magic Ring)

Turn Me On, gelded after two runs as a two-year-old, was partnered by Hayley Turner in his four remaining races for Michael Bell.

After the horses had worked on the gallops, Bell would ask the riders how their horse had gone. When it came to Turner, Bell asked, instead, what was she riding? He was hoping for the reply, 'Turn Me On, Guv'nor.' Bell recalled, sadly, 'She failed miserably to fall into the trap.'

Races won: six for trainer Tim Walford from 2007 to 2010.

BOUNCY BOUNCY (2007)
* Chineur * Wunderbra (Second Empire)

Trained by Michael Bell and usually ridden by Hayley Turner, Bouncy Bouncy won four times from 2010 to 2012, with Turner on board for three of the wins.

WUNDERBRA (2001)
* *Second Empire* * *Supportive (Nashamaa)*

Wunderbra won five times for Michael Bell in 2004 and 2005, with Hayley Turner responsible for four of the successes.

JUICY PEAR (2007)
* Pyrus * Cappadoce (General Monash)

As pears belong to the genus Pyrus, I may have got carried away. Juicy Pear won once for the Michael Bell–Hayler Turner combination, in 2010.

BRALESS (1974)
* Showoff II * Snuggles (Head Hunter)

Didn't get the support she needed, racing without success in New Zealand in 1979 and 1980.

BUSTED (1963)
• Crepello • Sans Le Sou (Vimy)

As Busted's dam was called Sans Le Sou – penniless – Busted's name was meant to mean busted in the sense of broke. Mischievous racehorse owners made other connections.

Once Busted's glittering racing career was replaced by life as a stallion, there were plenty of opportunities for exploiting his name, as well as that of his son Bustino and other descendants.

> Arguably a great champion, the best Flat horse trained in Britain in the 1960s.
> *John Randall's verdict on Busted, looking back in 2017*

Races won: 1966 Gallinule Stakes; 1967 Coronation Stakes, Eclipse Stakes, King George VI and Queen Elizabeth Stakes, Prix Henry Foy.

AMAZING BUST (1982)
• Busted • Amazer (Mincio)

Particularly amazing because Amazing Bust was a colt, which confused matters. In 1985 and 1986 he won four races in France.

FORTYTWO DEE (1990)
• Amazing Bust • Maggie's Way (Decent Fellow)

Fortytwo Dee was a filly who eventually, in 1998 and 2000, won two chases.

CLEAVAGE (1983)
• Hillandale • Divided (Busted)

Caro Balding, wife of trainer Toby Balding and initially owner of Cleavage, was said to harbour the ambition to hear a commentator declare, '... and Mrs Balding's Cleavage is out in front.'

Sadly, her Cleavage failed to match her ambition, proving on the woeful side both on the Flat and over hurdles from 1986 to 1988.

MISS THIRTYFOUR D (2000)
● Bertrando ● Fine Fettle (Sir Ivor)

Won at Hollywood Park in 2004 and at Santa Anita in 2005.

STRAPLESS (1979)
● Bustino ● Dame Foolish (Silly Season)

Won once in 1981 and ditto in 1982.

BUXOM LASS (1980)
● Bustino ● Lady From Aske (French Beige)

Only raced as a two-year-old. Possibly fell over forwards.

LINE ABREAST (1979)
● High Line ● Filiform (Reform)

If at first, etcetera – won on her 21st and final outing in 1984.

STIFF DICK

There was more than one Stiff Dick on the Turf, including a Royal Dick.

At Newmarket on 11 April 1698, King William III's Stiff Dick beat the highly regarded Careless in a match for The King's Plate.

In 1751, another Stiff Dick won at Winchester and Salisbury and, latterly called Little Janus, was exported to the USA in 1756 and was a winner there.

In 1806, a third Stiff Dick was odds-on favourite for a race for two-year-olds at Catterick, but bolted.

I expect you've assumed that all three Stiff Dicks have a sexual connotation. Shame on you! The use of the word 'dick' to mean 'penis' probably dates from the late nineteenth century, whereas Dick as shorthand for Richard is much older.

Sir Richard Onslow, Speaker of the House of Commons from 1708 to 1710, was known as 'Stiff Dick' because of his imperious and pedantic manner. Perhaps the Stiff Dick foaled in 1746 was named after him.

> The whole House referred to him as 'Stiff Dick' because of Sir Richard Onslow's 'unyielding insistence on the observation of proper protocol'.
> *Philip Marsden, The Officers of the Commons 1363–1965 (1966)*

Yet another name

O K Topless (2002)
• Old Topper • Ok Matt (Raised Socially)
Showed off successfully three times between 2004 and 2006, in Minnesota then California.

ISITINGOOD (1991)
• Crusader Sword • Wancha (Transworld)

Mike Pegram, who made his fortune from McDonald's franchises, has owned some top-of-the-tree racehorses, some on his own, others with Paul Weitman and Karl Watson. Trained by Bob Baffert, Real Quiet, bought by Pegram for $17,000, won the 1998 Kentucky Derby and Preakness Stakes before finishing second in the Belmont. Real Quiet also won three other Grade 1 races. Captain Steve won the 2001 Dubai World Cup, as well as three other Grade 1 races.

Then there was Silverbulletday, winner of the 1998 Breeders' Cup Juvenile Fillies and 1999 Kentucky Oaks, along with three other Grade 1 races, and Midnight Lute, who won the Breeders' Cup Sprint in 2007 and again the next year. Pegram had part-owned the winner of the same race in 1992, Thirty Slews.

And then there was Isitingood.

Pegram suggested that the name was based on that of the colt's sire, Crusader Sword but few believed him.

To make things worse, or better, Isitingood was a good horse. Between 1993 and 1997 he won 11 times, including four Graded Stakes races, and earned over $1.2 million.

A Jockey Club spokesman admitted, 'This is a name that we would prefer not to be in active use.' Unfortunately for the Jockey Club, it was too late.

Some uncomfortable track announcers chose to change Isitingood's name for the duration of their commentary. At Fair Grounds racetrack in 1997, race fans were led to believe that the winner was called Isn't It Good.

There's a statute of limitations on that one. When it's up,
I'll tell you how that name came about.
Mike Pegram when asked the origin of Isitingood's name

Quite a clever name

I'mallwilly (1999)
• *Walter Willy* • *I'm Linda (State Dinner)*
Won three times in unexalted company in California in 2002 and 2003.

JOHN WILKES – PART TWO (1970)
• Pall Mall • Ballerina (Preciptic)

You may be wondering where Part One is. It hasn't arrived yet – it's in chapter 16, and I suggest you read it first. Instead of complaining that the order's wrong you might give credit for novelty and innovation but I don't suppose you will.

John Wilkes belonged to the notorious Hellfire Club, a group of libertines led by Sir Francis Dashwood who met at Medmenham Abbey, leased by Dashwood in the mid-eighteenth century. Calling themselves the Order of the Knights of St Francis of Wycombe, they indulged in conversation, pranks, drinking and sex, usually in that order.

In 1759 Wilkes inherited a poem called 'An Essay on Woman' from fellow Club member Thomas Potter. It was a scurrilous parody of Alexander Pope's 'An Essay on Man'. Wilkes amended it and in 1763 printed a dozen copies, one of which, unfortunately for Wilkes, was read out in Parliament, where it was condemned as blasphemous and libellous. It contributed to Wilkes's expulsion from Parliament the following year.

'An Essay on Woman' has been called the dirtiest poem in the English Language. It reaches the extreme of indecorum, boundlessly bawdy, using every indecent word. *Arthur Cash,* John Wilkes: The Scandalous Father of Civil Liberty *(2006)*

Awake, my Fanny! Leave all meaner things;
This morn shall prove what raptures swiving brings!
Let us (since life can little more supply
Than just a few good fucks, and then we die)
Expatiate free o'er that lov'd scene of man,
A mighty maze! For mighty pricks to scan.
You get the idea. T. Potter and J. Wilkes, 'An Essay on Woman'

Races won: I can't add to what appears in chapter 16. None. Hopeless as a two-year-old in 1972; ditto in 1973.

Instructional names

Drop Your Drawers (1979)
* *Raise A Cup* • *Drapery (Bald Eagle)*
Raced in the USA, Drop Your Drawers won five times in 1981 and 1982, when he won two Grade 3 races and finished runner-up in the then Grade 1 Arlington Classic. He may have dropped his drawers but he pulled his socks up, unlike ...

Pull Your Socks Up (1999)
* *Needle Gun* • *Crackingham (Trimmingham)*
A failure under Rules and in point-to-points from 2004 to 2007.

DR RUSSELL COHEN

Like Caesar Kimmel (see section 9) and Mike Pegram, Dr Russell Cohen, a veterinarian, is prone to giving his horses ambiguous names. So...

DOUBLE DEE'S (1993)
* Double Negative • Oh How We Danced (Jinsky)

She won six times in 1995 and 1996, including at Grade 2 level. Cohen bred Double Dee's and she was owned by his mother Bernice's Tri-Bone Stables, so called because Cohen and his two brothers called each other 'bone-headed'.

WHAT A PEAR (2006)
* E Dubai • Perfect Pear (Pine Bluff)

She won four times during 2008 and 2009.

EFFINEX (2011)
● Mineshaft ● What A Pear (E Dubai)

When asked for the origin of the name Dr Cohen, who is divorced, acknowledged that it 'could refer to a certain person in my life', or alternatively to a German financial consultancy firm. I think we know which it was.

Effinex not only won nine races between 2014 and 2016, including three Grade 2 and one Grade 1 race, he also finished second to American Pharoah in the 2015 Breeders' Cup Classic. He earned over $3.3 million. It helped to pay for the divorce, I suppose.

ELLIE VON SHTUPP (2014)
● Awesome Gambler ● Sobresaliente (El Prado)

Ellie Von Shtupp ran only once and yet ran 11 times.

Inspired by Lili Von Shtupp, a character in Mel Brooks's 1974 film *Blazing Saddles*, the filly made her debut at Santa Anita on 15 January 2017. She finished unplaced but not unnoticed.

In a rare intervention after a horse has already raced, the American Jockey Club asked owner-breeder Terry Lovingier to change the three-year-old's name. A spokesman explained, 'We made the decision that the original name was approved in error.'

The Jockey Club's concern was not with the Ellie Von but with the Shtupp, a Yiddish word for having sex.

When Ellie Von Shtupp appeared at Santa Anita again the following month, she was Ellie Mae. Not everyone approved. Michael Wrona, the track announcer, tweeted, 'Sorry to report to her burgeoning fan base that the Jockey Club has frowned upon Ellie Von Shtupp. Henceforth, Ellie Mae.'

It didn't help her run faster. In 2018 she was still a maiden.

Hello, handsome, is that a ten-gallon hat or are you just enjoying the show?
Lili Von Shtupp (Madeline Kahn) in Blazing Saddles

10. COMMENTATORS' NIGHTMARES

To normal people, commentating would be a nightmare. Can you imagine calling the Stewards' Cup at Goodwood, with almost 30 runners charging out of the stalls and racing for six furlongs, taking only about 70 seconds?

As if the job isn't hard enough, some owners take a perverse delight in giving horses tricky names. In my youth I wanted to name a horse Andfinishingfast. In those days, before televisions were allowed in betting shops, customers relied on the commentaries supplied by Extel, the Exchange Telegraph Company. To foster suspense and keep up the hopes of favourite backers, commentators regularly announced '... and finishing fast ...' The name would probably fall foul of one of the Rules governing the naming of racehorses, the one that disallows names which 'may cause confusion in the administration of racing or betting'.

There are horses that have already achieved that.

ARRRRR (2004)
* Regal Classic * Lemons Ain't Limes (Bold Ruckus)

Arrrrr's victory in a claiming race at Saratoga in 2008 produced a memorable commentary by the legendary race caller Tom Durkin. It's worth looking up on YouTube.

Luckily, we are blessed with some brilliant commentators. Not only that, but you can watch horse races on television without the ubiquitous affliction of background music. I think that's why some people get to 70 and are ready to go, even at the risk of being tormented by singing and harp-playing in heaven.

Commentators aren't perfect, which is just as well because

it means that there's still scope to complain. Some are prone to shouting, sometimes a long way from the finish. Richard Hoiles and Simon Holt can plead not guilty to that, and are justifiably respected, but even their calm is occasionally tested.

Arrrrr, Arrrrr, Arrrrr gets to the front coming down to the wire. They're coming to the finish and it's all Arrrrr.
Tom Durkin

CUNNING STUNT (1969)
• Young Emperor • Jet Mist (Jet Pilot)

Caesar Kimmel (a great name until you consider what happened to Julius) started life as the son of a dubious father, Manny Kimmel. Manny was a big illegal New York bookmaker, early practitioner of card counting at blackjack and associate of Mafia figures. He also had parking lots in New York which Caesar inherited and eventually helped transform into Warner Communications Inc., later Time Warner.

As one of Warner's founders and until 1984 a senior executive, Caesar was able to indulge his liking for horseracing and tricky names. He excelled himself by naming a filly Cunning Stunt and sneaking her past the eyes of the American Jockey Club. She wasn't very good but in 1971 and 1972 was a regular in low-grade claiming races at New York tracks, racing about 30 times, mainly at Aqueduct.

Cunning Stunt won three times there in 1972 and as crowds of over 20,000 were commonplace, plenty of race fans were able to hear how the track announcers coped – sometimes with difficulty.

Perhaps it was no coincidence that the long-serving announcer Fred 'Cappy' Capossela retired at the end of 1971, to be replaced by his assistant, Dave Johnson. One race fan recalled, 'Cappy would almost come to a halt before he announced Cunning Stunt's racing position.'

If you run that horse at my track I'm going to call it by its number all the way around.

New York track announcer, probably Fred Capossela or Dave Johnson, during a phone call to Caesar Kimmel.

FLAT FLEET FEET (1993)
* Afleet • Czar Dancer(Czaravich)

Another of Caesar Kimmel's teases, Flat Fleet Feet was meant to trip up commentators, and sometimes did. From 1995 to 1997 there were 23 opportunities for her to do so. Flat Fleet Feet often figured prominently, winning seven times, including a Grade 2 race at Saratoga in 1995 and a Grade 1 race at Aqueduct in 1996.

Problematic names

Racehorse (2015)
* *Equiano • Lovely Dream (Elnadim)*
No one can deny that Racehorse is a racehorse. A £1,500 yearling, so far Racehorse has won once for TMBS Solutions Ltd and trainer Hughie Morrison.

Sec Secrets (1994)
* *Triple Sec • Sparkling Secret (Special Secret)*
Sec Secrets was employed to tease race callers, mainly at Texas tracks between 1996 and 1999. She won five times.

THE WINNER IS

To make things worse, there were two of them, guaranteed to upset race callers.

> ### THE WINNER IS (1993)
> • Academy Award • Miss Richard (Time for a Change)

Won at Philadelphia Park and Atlantic City in 1997.

> ### THE WINNER IS (2009)
> • West Acre • The Envelopeplease (Deputy Minister)

... at least had the decency to run only three times, winning on her debut at Calder in 2011.

RICHARD HOILES

Duckey Fuzz always filled me with trepidation. When I was younger Duckey Fuzz was a game played in a circle. You had to say Duckey Fuzz or Fuzzy Duck until someone slipped up. Then they had to drink a pint of beer.

When you have a tricky name you hope the horse runs badly and you don't have to mention it much. Winker Watson was horrible, because he was a good horse. When he ran at Royal Ascot I was petrified because the Queen was there.

Richard Hoiles

Races won: Duckey Fuzz (1988) won five times from 1991 to 1994; Winker Watson (2005) won three races, all as a two-year-old in 2007, including the Group 2 Norfolk Stakes at Royal Ascot and Group 2 July Stakes at Newmarket.

Richard Hoiles's names

Redlorryellowlorry (2011)

• *Bushranger* • *Bronze Baby (Silver Charm)*

Torture for children during elocution lessons, and much the same for commentators. Luckily Redlorryellowlorry wasn't very good, ran only nine times and won just once, at Brighton in 2014.

Roll-A-Joint (1978)

• *Take A Reef* • *Sark (Chamier)*

Developed into a cracking chaser, winning seven times during the 1988/89 season, climaxing with victory in the Scottish National. Altogether won a hurdle race and nine chases between 1984 and 1989.

Helawe (1983)

• *Last Fandango* • *Pigmy (Assagai)*

Based on a version of the joke about the Fukawi tribe of pygmies who jump up and down in the grasslands shouting, 'We're the Fukawi!' This version won 13 races from 1985 to 1991.

Near Kettering (2014)

• *Medicean* • *Where's Broughton (Cadeaux Genereux)*

To confuse things, not only is Broughton near Kettering but Near Kettering was bred by Michael Broughton. He won once, in 2017.

SIMON HOLT

You are under greater scrutiny nowadays, so thank goodness for Google and pronunciation websites. Mercifully, safety limits have come down, so you no longer have 30-runner maiden races at Redcar, which were really difficult because there were a lot of unfamiliar horses.

One horse that gave me a lot of trouble was Quantitativeeasing, who ran at eight successive

Cheltenham Festivals. It was the extra 't' that was the problem. Then there was Richard and Alison Guest's Udododontu and Udontdodou. I think some owners deliberately choose awkward names.
Simon Holt

Races won: despite his name, based on a method of increasing a country's money supply, Quantitativeeasing (2005) won eight races from 2009 to 2016, including a Grade 3 Chase at Cheltenham and two cross-country chases at Punchestown. Unfortunately for Holt, both Udododontu (2012) and Udontdodou (2013) often figured prominently. Udododontu won three times in 2015 and 2016 while Udontdodou won six times from 2016 to 2018.

Simon Holt's names

Hard To Handel (2012)
* *Stimulation* • *Melody Maker (Diktat)*
A cracking name. Won four races in England before moving to race in Jersey.

Cheeseandpickle (2015)
* *Helmet* • *Branston Gem (So Factual)*
Won on her debut as a two-year-old and has the future ahead of her, which is where the future tends to be.

Avril Etoile (1990)
* *Sharpo* • *Alsiba (Northfields)*
Born on 1 April, which should have been a warning, Simon Holt and others, including the author, bought Avril Etoile in 1993, by which time the Jack Holt-trained filly had already finished a narrowly beaten second three times. Regularly ridden by Iona Wands, Avril Etoile was genuine enough but not quite fast enough. By the time the partnership sold her, towards the end of 1994, she had been runner-up twice more and third five times. She never did win, in 37 attempts. C'est la vie.

11. MARKETING

AXMINSTER CARPETS

For about 20 years, from 1988 to 2007, Axminster Carpets raced horses bearing the names of their products. There was Royal Dartmouth and Royal Seaton, Royal Axminster and Royal Devon, Devonia Plains, Carpetsmadeindevon, Carpet Lady and Carpet Princess.

Harry Dutfield, the company chairman, liked horseracing and so did his son Simon, in charge from 1999. He liked it so much that he had been expelled from school for taking bets.

In 1990 Simon's wife Nerys took out a permit to train and five years later obtained a full licence, so that the equine carpets became part of the fabric of the family.

Evidently Axminster carpets are very good – I suppose I must have trodden on some of them – and although the company's horses were less distinguished they mustered a decent tally of small race successes. Royal Dartmouth, Royal Seaton, Royal Axminster and Carpet Princess won 14 races between them and perhaps some of those who backed them bought new carpets with their winnings.

An insulting name

Miss Rubbish (1978)

• Rubor • Mishwish (Indian Ruler)

Despite being a non-thoroughbred, she wasn't rubbish, blossoming for a season in 1985/86 when she won four jumps races and finished third in the 1986 Scottish National.

To add insult to injury, two of Miss Rubbish's offspring, half-sisters, were named *Little Idiot* (1991) and *Trivial (1992)*.

> **DONCASTER ROVER (2006)**
> • War Chant • Rebridled Dreams (Unbridled's Song)

The fans – Peter Holling, Ian Raeburn and Steve Halsall – who owned Doncaster Rover were probably trying to save the club money by leaving out the closing 'S'. Or maybe they thought that the ploy would attract attention and with it promotion.

For a long time Doncaster Rovers were best known for the size of their Belle Vue pitch, the biggest in the UK, their memorable 1946/47 season, when they were League Division Three (North) champions, and for the unfulfilled talent of Alick Jeffrey.

Jeffrey made his debut as a 15-year-old in 1954 and scored 15 goals in 13 games in the 1956/57 season before breaking his leg when playing for the England Under-23 side against France, aged 17. Told he would never play again, Jeffrey made an emotional comeback at Belle Vue in 1963. He wasn't the player he could have been but still scored 36 goals the following season.

As a horse Doncaster Rover, carrying Doncaster Rovers' red and white colours, did the club proud. Bought for 35,000 guineas as a yearling, he won over £200,000, although he never won at Doncaster. Still, Doncaster Rovers often don't win there, either.

> Ronaldo could play for Millwall, QPR, Doncaster Rovers
> or anyone and he'd score a hat-trick.
> *Sir Alex Ferguson, 2015. I wish he would.*

Races won: five, including three Listed races in 2009, 2010 and 2011.

> **BELLE VUE (1973)**
> • Track Spare • Royal Camp (Sovereign Path)

It would be nice to think that the horse was named after Doncaster Rovers' ground, or at least Wakefield Trinity Rugby League Club's ground of the same name. Not so!

Belle Vue was initially owned and trained by Ron Mason. Mason had been a speedway rider and started his career at the Belle Vue track in Manchester. He named the horse after that.

One year at Royal Ascot I rode two apparent no-hopers for Ron Mason, at 100-9 and 33-1. Such was his charisma and confidence that by the time I left the paddock he had convinced me that they would both win – and they did! *Jockey Jimmy Lindley looking back to 1966, when Track Spare won the St James's Palace Stakes and, the next day, Petite Path won the Queen Mary Stakes.*

Races won: Belle Vue was given plenty of chances – he ran 157 times between 1975 and 1985. He won nine races on the Flat, the last when he was a 12-year-old, and one over hurdles.

Strange names for horses

Coal Bunker (1978)
• *On Your Mark* • *Powder Box (Faberge II)*
Wasn't black or even grey but chestnut. Battled on regardless to win twice on the Flat and once over hurdles between 1980 and 1982.

Dishcloth (1974)
• *Fury Royal* • *Drishouge (Straight Deal)*
Wiped the floor (sorry) with her opponents in five hurdle races and four chases between 1981 and 1985.

GEARY'S

It's a bit of a mystery. If you lived in Wolverhampton in the 1970s and 1980s the name Henry Geary might mean something to you, particularly if you worked in the steel industry and especially if you worked for H. Geary Ltd.

In 1978 Wolverhampton staged the H. Geary Ltd Nursery Handicap and in 1981 it staged the H. Geary Ltd Handicap Chase, strong evidence that H. Geary existed.

Steel manufacturing isn't a romantic field and Geary's horses didn't bear romantic names. Geary's For Strip, Geary's For Steel, Geary's Steel Stock, Gearys Cold Rolled and, by way of a change, Henry Geary Steels. The message was clear – the message was Geary. Between 1978 and 1990 the Geary string carried the name of Geary far and wide.

Whether, with the steel industry in decline, they helped to sell Geary's steel is doubtful. Today, Geary appears to have gone. Maybe it's moved to China; they make a lot of steel there.

Races won: nothing magnificent but Gearys Cold Rolled won nine times over jumps, Henry Geary Steels won six times ditto and Geary's For Strip won four races on the Flat. Good for Geary.

HINARI

Hinari Consumer Electronics Limited was established by Brian Palmer in 1985. Two years later, at Carlisle, *Hinari Video (1985) Sallust – Little Cynthia (Wolver Hollow)* gave trainer Mark Johnston his first winner.

The stable soon included Hinari Hi Fi, Hinari Sound, Hinari Sunrise, Hinari Televideo, Hinari Disk Deck and Hinari Vision. It was a brief Hinari flurry. The company was sold in 1989 and although that year Hinari Sunrise won the Bibury Cup at Salisbury and Hinari Televideo won the William Hill Handicap at Royal Ascot in the company's colours, most of the horses' successes came for other owners.

Hinari Video was of modest ability but tremendously durable. Between 1987 and 1995 he won 13 times from 134 appearances. In 1992, as a seven-year-old, he ran 34 times. Only his first success was for the Hinari company.

A custard name

Bird's Custard (1976)

• *Birdbrook* • *Dairy Queen (Queen's Hussar)*
As an egg-free custard, invented by Alfred Bird in 1837, a commercial
triumph; as a racehorse, not so much. She did win a race at Edinburgh
in 1978, which is one more than most racehorses manage.

> Buy Best! Buy Bird's! Buy British!
> Bird's is the nutritious custard – that is why it is so good for
> growing children.
> *1932 advertisement*

LAKER

More flamboyant than Fred Pontin
(see below), Freddie Laker was the
trailblazer for low-cost airlines.
Managing director of British United
Airways from 1960 to 1965, Laker
founded Laker Airways in 1966
and battled fierce obstruction,
particularly from bigger rivals, to
offer cut-price airfares. By then he
had developed a passion for racing,

bought Woodcote Stud and in 1965 won the Triumph Hurdle with
Blarney Beacon (1961) Ballymoss – Fluorescent (Blue Peter).

After years of commercial and legal warfare, in 1977 Laker
launched Skytrain, offering cut-price transatlantic flights. Laker
was an energetic promoter and, like Pontin, saw the marketing
potential of racehorses. Take A Laker, raced in 1976 and 1977,
was hopeless but in 1977 Go Laker won three times and in 1978,
when Laker was knighted for services to the airline industry,
Go Skytrain followed suit.

In 1980 Skytrain Hostess won a maiden race at Salisbury and the following year Skytrain Jetset flew the flag, albeit without winning. In 1982 Laker Airways went bankrupt and Woodcote Stud was sold.

By then Sir Freddie Laker had, rather surprisingly, been elected to the Jockey Club. In the early 1980s he served as a racecourse steward at both Lingfield and Brighton.

Laker died in 2006, aged 83.

> Sir Freddie Laker may be at peace with his maker
> but he is persona non grata with IATA.
> *Prince Philip. IATA is the International Air*
> *Transport Association.*

Races won: Blarney Beacon 1965 Triumph Hurdle.

PONTIN

In 1946 Fred Pontin opened a holiday camp at Brean Sands, between Burnham-on-Sea and Weston-super-Mare. It is still open today. Upmarket from his rival Billy Butlin's camps, Pontin expanded rapidly and in 1963 formed Pontinental to set up holiday villages abroad.

The generally unsmiling entrepreneur saw the potential of racehorses for marketing the Pontin brand. His first horse was called Go-Pontin, followed by Pontin-Go and Go-Pontinental. Jockeys were instructed to race prominently so that 'Pontin' featured frequently in the race commentary.

Go-Pontin was noteworthy because, as Gay Navarree, he had finished fourth in the 1962 Grand National. Two years later Pontin bought Gay Navarree, changed its name and ran him in the 1964, 1965 and 1966 Grand Nationals. By then Go-Pontin was 14 and was replaced as Pontin's Aintree representative by Go-Pontinental, who finished second in the 1967 Topham Chase but fell in the 1968 Grand National.

In 1971 Pontin won the Schweppes Gold Trophy with Cala Mesquida, named after the resort Pontin owned in Majorca. Less than two months later he would have won the Grand National with Specify-Pontin, but was thwarted by a Jockey Club Rule preventing such changes of name, so won the race with Specify.

By 1975 Pontins owned 25 holiday villages, the largest with 5,000 beds, and the company made a profit that year of £3.6 million (£27.7 million today). The following year Pontin was knighted for his charity work. In 1978 he sold the business, which was later owned by Trevor Hemmings, a much bigger racehorse owner, for £56 million (£295 million today).

Pontin's name still appears at racecourses, as a race sponsor.

When I take up golf or buy myself a yacht, see that I am certified.
Sir Fred Pontin, not noted for his joie de vivre, *continued to be engaged by business into old age. He died in 2000, aged 93.*

Races won: Go-Pontin 1965 Eider Chase; Cala Mesquida 1971 Schweppes Gold Trophy; Specify 1971 Grand National.

SEAGRAM (1980)
• Balak • Llanah (Bally Royal)

In the early 1980s, when Aintree was owned by the controversial property developer Bill Davies, the Grand National was in danger of coming to an end – again. A public appeal failed to raise enough money to buy Aintree and the course was saved, in part at least, by the intervention of Major Ivan Straker, chief executive of Seagram, a Canadian distillery company.

A racing enthusiast, Straker persuaded his boss to bridge the gap between what had been raised and Davies's asking price and subsequently to sponsor the Grand National. 'I rang up my boss in New York, Edgar Bronfman,' Straker recalled, 'and said, "Listen, you've always wanted to raise the profile of Seagram in the United Kingdom, and here is the most wonderful, wonderful chance."' From 1984 to 1991 it was the Seagram Grand National.

To complete the marketing coup, in 1991 the race was won
by Seagram.

A small horse but an accurate and economical jumper, Seagram
was reminiscent of Red Rum. His victory was not universally
welcome. Seagram was the author's ante-post selection for the
National. Unfortunately, having missed 33-1, by the time he had
cursed himself for that he had also missed the 25-1 and 20-1 and
was too irritated to take 16-1. By the day of the race, when Seagram
was 12-1, the idiot author simply hoped that he wouldn't win. You
may know the feeling.

Sod it.
David Ashforth, shortly after Seagram's five-length triumph

Races won: a wonderfully bonny and giving horse, Seagram not
only won the 1991 Grand National but also the same year's National
Hunt Handicap Chase at the Cheltenham Festival, plus nine other
chases and four hurdles.

A waspish name

Duke Of Waspington (2013)
• Duke Of Marmalade • Queen Wasp (Shamardal)
Nicely named and although winless so far, there is still hope.

SIZING

If Alan Potts had been a baker, his horses might have been called
Flapjack or Bakewell Tart (except that those names were already
taken) but he was an engineer who made a fortune from developing
sizing machines for crushing and grading coal, so he named them
after that.

In 1978, Potts founded Mining Machinery Developments,
which sold sizing machines around the world and later
manufactured them in Africa and China as well as the UK. It was

very good for Alan and Ann Potts but not so good when it came to giving their many racehorses imaginative names.

There was Sizing Mexico and Sizing Canada, Sizing Italy and Sizing Venezuela, Sizing Chile, Sizing Brisbane and Sizing Rome. Not all the Potts's horses were called Sizing something but over 40 of them were.

The Potts's green and yellow colours, topped by a red cap, became a familiar sight, initially through the exploits of Sizing Europe, who won 22 jumps races and over £1.3 million in prize money between 2006 and 2014.

I don't know how much the Potts paid Hugh Bleahen for Sizing Europe but Bleahen had bought him as a foal for just €9,000. The Bleahens were good at it because eight years later, in 2010, John Bleahen bought another foal for €16,000 and sold it to the Potts. They called it Sizing John, who won the 2017 Cheltenham Gold Cup.

Later on, there were much more expensive buys. In February 2017, a few days after Flemenshill won a six-runner maiden point-to-point at Oldtown in Ireland, he was bought on the Potts's behalf for £480,000. It's a ridiculous amount for a four-year-old gelding and, sadly, neither Ann nor Alan lived to see Flemenshill run. Both died later that year as, unfortunately, did Flemenshill.

It's the first horse we have ever run in the Gold Cup, and only a couple of weeks after we won the Irish Gold Cup with Sizing John. Pretty good.
Alan Potts after Sizing John won the 2017 Cheltenham Gold Cup

Races won: lots – 22 by Sizing Europe, eight of them Grade 1 races, including 2008 Irish Champion Hurdle, 2010 Arkle Chase, 2011 Queen Mother Champion Chase and Tingle Creek Chase, 2012 and 2014 Irish Champion Chase. So far, Sizing John has won nine races, including five Grade 1 events, among them the 2017 Irish Gold Cup, Cheltenham Gold Cup and Punchestown Gold Cup.

Sizing Coal (2008)
* *Presenting • Hollygrove Cezanne (King's Ride)*

Naming a horse after a process for crushing coal is not, marketing aside, appealing. To be fair, Sizing Coal has won four chases and three point-to-points.

Sizing Granite (2008)
* *Milan • Hazel's Tisrara (Mandalus)*

As bad a name as Sizing Coal. He has still won five chases and two hurdles so far, which is a tribute to his strength of character.

Sizing Machine (2008)
* *King's Theatre • Sno Cat Lady (Executive Perk)*

A terrible name for a horse, even if horses are sometimes referred to as 'machines'. They shouldn't be. He overcame the adversity to win twice over jumps.

12. HOW THE BIG NAMES CHOOSE NAMES

THE QUEEN

Breeding and racing horses is the Queen's passion and has been throughout her long reign. Her colours – purple, gold braid, scarlet sleeves, black velvet cap with gold fringe – were carried to Classic success by Carrozza in the 1957 Oaks and by Pall Mall in the following year's 2,000 Guineas. In 1974 Highclere won the 1,000 Guineas and Prix de Diane, while Dunfermline triumphed in the 1977 Oaks and St Leger.

The Queen has not been immune from the usual, inevitable snakes and ladders experiences of ownership, its pleasant and unpleasant surprises. Along the way there have been plenty of happy days, not least when Estimate, described by trainer Sir Michael Stoute as 'a pain in the backside at times', won the 2013 Ascot Gold Cup. It is considered unseemly for a monarch to leap up and down shouting, 'Go on, my son!' but the Queen's delight, expressed in a less demonstrative fashion, was apparent.

It was the first time the historic race had been won by a reigning monarch. As the race was first run in 1807, eight of Queen Elizabeth II's forerunners had been – in regard to the Ascot Gold Cup – comparative failures.

Given her enduring love of horses, it is not surprising that she takes the lead in naming them.

'She does the naming herself,' says John Warren, the Queen's long serving bloodstock and racing adviser. 'There used to be about 15 horses to be named each year but that number is now up to about 25.

'It's something she'll pick up and consider on a number of occasions, usually starting to think about names for the foals in August when she's at Balmoral. She'll sometimes ask guests if they have suggestions based on a horse's pedigree. She knows the families and will try to find a name with a connection to the pedigree but, slightly frustratingly, a lot of names are not available. If there isn't a suitable name based on the pedigree, she'll come up with another nice name.'

One rather nice one was *Mustard (2012) Motivator – Flash Of Gold (Darshaan)*, who proved keen enough to win three races, including the 2015 Old Rowley Cup at Newmarket.

PRINCE KHALID ABDULLAH

Every race fan recognises Prince Khalid Abdullah's colours: green, with a pink sash, white sleeves, pink cap – the colours worn by Known Fact, Rainbow Quest, Dancing Brave, Banks Hill, Frankel and many other top-class horses. The colours were chosen on the recommendation of Lord Weinstock, himself a major racehorse owner and breeder, because they were the colours of Prince Khalid's curtains.

Khalid Abdullah has been a major player on the international racing scene for 40 years. His first winner was Charming Native in a small race at Windsor in 1979. Later, he preferred to breed rather than buy his horses and Juddmonte Farms, his breeding operation, produces foals on an intimidating scale for Prince Khalid and those helping to name them.

That includes racing manager Lord 'Teddy' Grimthorpe, who sounds like a heartless coal owner in a Charles Dickens novel but seems to have survived aristocracy and emerged as a good egg.

Naming Prince Khalid's horses is a never-ending process. Trying to find names for 160 to 180 horses a year is tricky, especially when so many names aren't available. We have an in-house competition to be won by staff who come up with names that are actually chosen.

We have to assemble names that are available in the US, France, Ireland and Britain, then get horses named as quickly as possible in one country in case they move to another. We try to get them all named by 1 December each year.

All the names are approved by Prince Khalid. We submit a choice of names that are going to be acceptable to the authorities and he chooses. He likes to name the horses we hope will be the best himself. The best tend to be approved last. Frankel wasn't named until March.

Prince Khalid likes short, memorable names, and with colts who are hopefully going to make stallions it does matter to have suitable names, although a good racehorse becomes a good name.

Lord 'Teddy' Grimthorpe in his own words (more or less)

If you have read previous chapters, you may feel that some names could never become good names.

The Elvis connection

Neither Prince Khalid nor Lord Grimthorpe are noted Elvis Presley fans but his 1962 hit 'Return to Sender' struck a chord at Juddmonte Farms. 'Prince Khalid indulged me,' says Grimthorpe. 'It was a bit of fun.'

I gave a letter to the postman, he put it in his sack.
Bright 'n' early next morning, he brought my letter back.
She wrote upon it
'Return to sender. Address unknown.
No such number. No such zone.'

We had a quarrel, a lovers' spat,
I write I'm sorry, but my letter keeps coming back.
Elvis Presley, 'Return to Sender'

Return (1997)

• *Sadler's Wells* • *Slightly Dangerous (Roberto)*

Won a maiden race on her debut in 2000. Three races later she was off to stud.

To Sender (2003)

• *King's Best* • *Return (Sadler's Wells)*

Won on his debut at Newbury in 2005 and, sent to join trainer Bobby Frankel in the US, won twice at Santa Anita in 2006.

Coming Back (2006)

• *Fantastic Light* • *Return (Sadler's Wells)*

Won once in 2009.

Address Unknown (2007)

• *Oasis Dream* • *Return (Sadler's Wells)*

Won three times on the Flat in Ireland between 2009 and 2011 when trained by Dermot Weld. He was then sold and won twice more, including the 2013 Chester Cup.

No Such Number (2008)

• *King's Best* • *Return (Sadler's Wells)*

Won six races between 2012 and 2017, five of them over jumps, but none in Khalid Abdullah's colours. He sold No Such Number in 2011.

No Such Zone (2011)

• *Oasis Dream* • *Return (Sadler's Wells)*

Unraced and sold in 2017.

COOLMORE

The Coolmore Goliath, with John Magnier's big brain inside it, is unlikely to suffer the same fate as the biblical colossus and be felled by David's sling.

The breeding and racing operation, the latter in the capable hands of Aidan O'Brien at Ballydoyle, is to the horseracing industry what the New England Patriots, Bill Belichick and Tom Brady are to American football. They're not very popular with some people, either.

Applying an impressive list of commercial assets, such as strong leadership, sound organisation, extensive knowledge, political influence and lots of money, Coolmore has turned some of the best racehorses in the world into some of the best stallions.

Susan Magnier, John's wife, chooses the names to be bestowed on each year's new inmates and it is no coincidence that most of Coolmore's best horses, especially the colts, have the most distinguished names. They wouldn't want one of their duds to be called Camelot, while their next Derby winner and stallion prospect was called Who Gives A Donald (see section 9).

Successful naming involves identifying the best horses early and reserving suitably exalted names for use when a potentially top-class one emerges. The names are rarely inspired by those of the horse's parents.

Camelot was reputed to have been stored in Sue Magnier's diary for almost ten years before a 2009 foal by Montjeu out of Tarfah was deemed worthy of the name. He won the 2011 Racing Post Trophy and 2012 2,000 Guineas, Derby and Irish Derby. Good choice!

The Magniers are averse to interviews but after Ruler Of The World won the 2013 Derby (the fourth of six for Coolmore/ Ballydoyle so far), John Magnier said, 'All the horses are rated on pedigree, then rated as individuals. Sue names all the horses in February/March time. Aidan gives his thoughts from week to week. This horse obviously made his way to the top. Sometimes they get it right, sometimes they don't. We've had a lot of bad American presidents.' Magnier was probably thinking of the human ones, because George Washington the horse did well, although John F. Kennedy was a disappointment.

Sue Magnier's mother, Jacqueline O'Brien, was born

in Australia and when the horse of that name won the 2014 Derby Tom Magnier, John and Sue's son, said, 'There was a strong determination to ensure that the name "Australia" was given to a colt considered capable of going right to the very top.' He did, going on to win the Irish Derby and Juddmonte International.

Punters are advised to look out for suitably named juveniles, in the tradition of King Of Kings, Stravinsky, Mozart, the mighty Galileo, Yeats, Dylan Thomas, George Washington, Beethoven, Camelot, Australia and Ruler Of The World.

LISTEN (2005)
• Sadler's Wells • Brigid (Irish River)

I thought the Coolmore filly, who won the 2007 Group 1 Fillies' Mile at Ascot, must have been named after one of Aidan O'Brien's favourite words. Sadly, she wasn't. Life's full of disappointments.

JOSEPH O'BRIEN

The son of a famous father does well to make his own distinctive mark, especially if working in the same field.

Joseph, son of Aidan O'Brien, made his mark as a multiple-Classic-winning Irish champion jockey. When he turned to training in 2016, aged just 23, he made an immediate impact and the following year became the youngest trainer ever to win the Melbourne Cup, with Rekindling. Then Joseph showed that he belonged to the age of social media by turning to Twitter to name a horse.

'It can be hard to come up with names,' said O'Brien. 'When you're training horses there are a lot of other things to be concentrating on without spending time on names.' So he invited his followers on Twitter to suggest a name for a four-year-old filly by *Presenting – Rare Gesture (Shalford)*.

To the trainer's amazement, over 3,000 suggestions appeared, and when O'Brien reduced them to a short list of four, over 9,000 votes were cast to choose the winner. The filly was related to top-class hurdlers Rhinestone Cowboy and Wichita Lineman, both named after Glen Campbell songs, and three of the four shortlisted candidates – I'll Be Me, Galveston Girl and A Lady Like You – had Glen Campbell connections.

The odd one out, chosen simply because O'Brien liked the name, was Seldom Is Precious and that was the winner. 'It's a lovely name,' said O'Brien, 'and I'm delighted with it.'

> We didn't have electricity when I was a kid. We had
> to watch TV by candlelight.
> *Glen Campbell, 2008*

Races won: give Seldom Is Precious a chance. She hasn't run yet.

SHEIKH MOHAMMED

Jan Gardner has worked for Sheikh Mohammed and Godolphin for decades and has been closely involved in choosing names for thousands of horses. Now the Racing Office Manager at the Godolphin Management Company, Gardner says, 'I've done a lot of it. I enjoy it. It's a research-based sort of job where you have to be creative. The main problem is the availability of names. You find a brilliant name then discover that it's already gone.'

Sometimes a competition is held among the staff for the best name for a horse and occasionally an archivist from the Royal Household has played a part. It was an archivist who suggested *Halling (1991) Diesis – Dance Machine (Green Dancer)*. Halling is a Norwegian folk dance, as well as the two-time winner of both the Group 1 Coral Eclipse Stakes (1995 and 1996) and Group 1 Juddmonte International (ditto), plus the 1996 Group 1 Prix d'Ispahan.

'Ideally,' says Gardner, 'we try to match the sire and dam – for example, *Plea Bargain (2002)* was by Machiavellian out of Time Saved.' In a racing career spanning only six races and less than

a year, Plea Bargain won three times, including the 2005 Group 2
King Edward VII Stakes.

Then there was *African Story (2007) Pivotal – Blixen (Gone West)*.
Karen Blixen was the celebrated Danish author of *Out of Africa*
(1937), based on her life in Kenya. Blixen would have been pleased to
see African Story win the 2014 Dubai World Cup, seven other races
and almost £5 million in prize money. Sadly, Blixen died in 1962.

DUBAI MILLENNIUM (1996)
* Seeking The Gold • Colorado Dancer (Shareef Dancer)

In 1998, one of Sheikh Mohammed's two-year-olds was called
Yaazer. The big bay colt was living at David Loder's Sefton Lodge
Stables in Newmarket. Loder thought that the unraced Yaazer
might turn out to be the best horse he had trained. 'I'm going to
change his name,' Sheikh Mohammed told Loder. 'I'm going to
call him Dubai Millennium.'

It was a very good choice. Dubai Millennium was brilliant on
turf and brilliant on dirt. He was beaten only once in his ten races,
when stepped up to one and a half miles for the Derby.

> That was the best day ever in racing for me. When you call
> a horse Dubai Millennium and he wins the Dubai World
> Cup in 2000, that is just great.
> *Sheikh Mohammed*

> Dubai Millennium was a very special horse for me, for us,
> for everybody. You could see his big heart in his eyes, you
> could see the wind blow between his ears when he ran. He
> was something different.
> *Sheikh Mohammed*

Races won: 1999 Group 1 Prix Jacques le Marois and Group 1 Queen
Elizabeth II Stakes; 2000 Group 1 Dubai World Cup and Group 1
Prince of Wales's Stakes.

GODOLPHIN (1980)
• Godswalk • Lilgarde (Hugh Lupus)

Maybe he'd have tried harder and been less temperamental if he'd realised that, over 200 years earlier, Godolphin Arabian, along with the Byerley Turk and Darley Arabian, would form the seeds from which all today's thoroughbreds descend.

Godolphin might also have run faster if he'd known that in 1993 his name would be the one chosen by Sheikh Mohammed for his bold plan to bring Dubai to Europe and that, in 1994, Godolphin's royal blue colours would be registered in Britain.

But he didn't know, and settled for winning three small races in 1983 and 1984.

13. THE ARTS AND SCIENCES

AGATHA CHRISTIE (2010)
● Pure Prize ● Amaya (American Chance)

This particular Agatha Christie won three races in Argentina in 2014. Other Agatha Christies, as befits an author translated into over 100 languages, have raced in Germany and New Zealand. There should be an English one but doesn't seem to have been.

Whatever the language, in Christie's detective novels someone can be relied upon to get murdered, while either Hercule Poirot or Miss Marple can be relied upon to expose the murderer. Killers have no chance in books by Agatha Christie (1890–1976), who vies with William Shakespeare for the title of all-time bestselling fiction author – and Shakespeare (1564–1616) had a 300-year start.

Amazingly, Christie's play *The Mousetrap*, first staged in the West End in 1952, is still alive there today, although some of the characters are dead.

Agatha Christie supplied her own mystery in 1926 when suddenly disappearing. Her husband Archibald, involved with another woman, had asked for a divorce. There was a nationwide womanhunt, which eventually revealed that Christie was staying at the Swan Hydropathic Hotel (now the Old Swan Hotel) in Harrogate.

She had signed in under the name of Mrs Teresa Neele. Her husband's mistress was Nancy Neele. I stayed there myself in 2005. Agatha had left and the hotel was very run-down, making me wish someone would find Christie and ask her to send Miss Marple along to see if she could find any hot water because I couldn't. Several years later the hotel changed hands and was modernised.

HERCULE POIROT (1987)
• Law Society • Welsh Berry (Sir Ivor)

The Belgian detective used 'the little grey cells' to solve every mystery he was presented with. David Suchet's rendering of Poirot was so popular that the television series ran for over 20 years (1989–2013).

Personally, I find the conceited character with a waxed moustache irritating, along with his mannerisms. I am not alone: Agatha Christie came to despise him, describing him as 'an egocentric creep'. Unfortunately, although everyone else in her books was susceptible to being killed, Poirot was immune, on the grounds that he was making fortunes for the author and her publishers.

> Rest assured, I am the best!
> *The insufferable Hercule Poirot in* Five Little Pigs *(1942)*

Races won: just the one, at Philadelphia Park in 1991. So he wasn't as clever as he thought.

ORIENT EXPRESS (1979)
• Blues Traveller • Oriental Splendour (Runnett)

The owner missed out the beginning – 'Murder on the' – which was unforgivable because it would have had too many letters.

Murder on the Orient Express appeared as a book in 1934 and a film in 1974, with Albert Finney playing Poirot. Remakes of films are usually a mistake, but the 2017 version, with Kenneth Branagh as Poirot, is excellent.

Well, almost excellent. The trouble is that there are so many characters to introduce that by the time they have been, the audience's patience (mine, anyway) is wearing thin. For the next remake, perhaps they should kill off a few passengers before they board the train.

The body, the cage, is everything of the most respectable,
but through the bars, the wild animal looks out.
Hercule Poirot's view of Samuel Ratchett, Murder on the
Orient Express

Races won: failed to run like its namesake, losing in 16 attempts
between 2000 and 2002.

MISS MARPLE (2006)
• Saarland • Future Diamonds (Roberto)

Several actresses have played the nosy Miss Jane Marple, mainly
on television, but the splendid Margaret Rutherford was the first
to bring her to life outside Agatha Christie's novels.

In Britain, the equine
Miss Marple (1997) failed to
reach the winning post first
in nine outings. Namesakes
also raced in Germany, South
Africa and New Zealand
but, surprisingly, it was in
Oklahoma, Louisiana and
Arkansas that she found success.

> **Miss Marple:** 'Oh, Miss Milchrest, good morning. How
> nice to see you again.'
> **Miss Milchrest** (apparently frightened): 'Good morning.'
> **Miss Marple:** 'Don't look so frightened, my dear. I've done
> my quota of murders for today.'
> *In the film* Murder at the Gallop *(1963)*

Races won: three, all in 2010, at Oaklawn Park, Louisiana Downs
and Remington Park.

THE MOUSETRAP (2013)
• Western Winter • Field Mouse (Badger Land)

Whereas the play has clocked up over 27,000 performances, its equine impersonator managed just four poor ones, all in South Africa in 2016.

A medical name

Trust Me I'm A Dr (2009)
• Dr Massini • Friendly Flick (Anshan)
Better not. Showing extraordinary confidence in his own ability, in 2018 the Doctor launched himself into racing under Rules on the back of 15 undistinguished appearances in point-to-points. In his first nine starts, Trust Me I'm A Dr, starting at 50-1 once, 66-1 once, 100-1 twice, 150-1 three times and 200-1 twice, was pulled up six times, finished last of six, last of four finishers and last of five finishers. Owner-trainer Victor Thompson said, 'I quite like him, and think he's better than he has shown.' Hmmm.

BEATRIX POTTER (2005)
• Cadeaux Genereux • Great Joy (Grand Lodge)

Horses don't feature prominently, if at all, in Beatrix Potter's classic collection of children's stories. Rabbits, hedgehogs, frogs and mice are regulars but not horses. Potter (1866–1943) was much keener on sheep, which she bred with distinction on her farm in the Lake District.

So her failure as a racehorse was perhaps to be expected, as was the appearance of several of her characters in racehorse form. They didn't fare too well, either.

> Once upon a time there were four little Rabbits, and their names were – Flopsy, Mopsy, Cotton-tail and Peter.
> *The Tale of Peter Rabbit (1902)*

Races won: regrettably, none, from 15 tries in Ireland between 2007 and 2009.

PETER RABBIT (1975)
• Double Jump • Peterkin (Blue Peter)

Would have done better in Mr McGregor's garden. A flop in three races in 1977 and 1978. Not big enough, I suppose.

MR MCGREGOR (1982)
• Formidable • Mrs Tiggywinkle (Silly Season)

... and

MR MCGREGOR (2008)
• Beneficial • Our Idol (Mandalus)

The 1982 version won two small races in 1986 and 1987, unlike the 2008 version, who failed to win under Rules. Mr McGregor had a rough time of it. First Peter Rabbit ate his vegetables, then he failed to flourish as a horse.

SQUIRREL NUTKIN (1998)
• Bluebird • Saltoki (Ballad Rock)

As a squirrel, memorable, as a racehorse, immemorable. Few people now remember his 16 successive defeats in 2000 and 2001. Perhaps, like his namesake, he was a bit of a rascal. I wonder if he also lost his tail.

MRS TIGGYWINKLE (1971)
• *Silly Season* • *My Enigma (Klairon)*

... and

> ### MRS TIGGYWINKLE (1998)
> ● Magic Ring ● Upper Sister (Upper Case)

Rather like remakes of classic films, it is often a mistake for a character to be resurrected. Mrs Tiggywinkle (1971 vintage) only won once, but at least it was at Goodwood, in 1973. Mrs Tiggywinkle (1998 version) ran 26 times from 2000 to 2002, but to no avail.

> ### JEREMY FISHER (1991)
> ● Ardross ● Ovington Court (Prefairy)

Well qualified to leap and won a hunter chase in 1999. That was it, on the winning front, although he did only run twice.

> ### MISS MOPPET (2011)
> ● Nayef ● So Blissful (Cape Cross)

No good, I'm afraid: nought from eight in 2014 and 2015.

> ### SAMUEL WHISKERS (1997)
> ● Son Pardo ● Yah Dancer (Shareef Dancer)

Nope, another disappointment: nought from six in 1999. It's just as well that Samuel Whiskers' creator wasn't alive to endure it. As a rat, and a rather fat one, he wasn't going to win the Derby or Cheltenham Gold Cup, was he?

> ### MR TOD (1998)
> ● Mistertopogigo ● Pillow Talk (Taufan)

Maybe if he'd tried more than five times he might have won something. No, he wouldn't have done.

TOM KITTEN (1981)
• Upton • Kellykitten (Nothing To Say)

... and

TOM KITTEN (2007)
• Kitten's Joy • Coax Classic (Caveat)

About time. The 1981 one, raced exclusively at Assiniboia racetrack in Winnipeg, Manitoba, won 16 times between 1983 and 1989. Admittedly, the races were humble ones – Tom Kitten earned less than $50,000 for his achievements.

The 2007 one, racing in in the USA, won ten times between 2010 and 2014, earning over $200,000. Maybe other Beatrix Potter characters should have moved to North America.

MRS TITTLEMOUSE (1980)
• Nonoalco • Lady Mouse (Sir Ivor)

... and

MRS TITTLEMOUSE (2003)
• Montjeu • Nuance (Star Way)

Mrs Tittlemouse the first seems never to have raced, while Mrs Tittlemouse the second, bred in New Zealand, won three races there in 2008 and 2009. Maybe other Beatrix Potter characters should have moved to New Zealand.

JEMIMA PUDDLEDUCK (1991)
• Tate Gallery • Tittlemouse (Castle Keep)

Well done, Jemima. Four wins from 37 tries between 1993 and 1997. It's not wonderful, but it's better than most.

BETJEMAN (2015)
• Poet's Voice • Respectfilly (Mark Of Esteem)

John Betjeman (1906–84) was one of the most loved and accessible poets and broadcasters of the twentieth century.

Not an obvious candidate for running fast, or at all, Betjeman did appreciate railways, although it was not the speed of the trains that appealed to his endearing, idiosyncratic nature. If you haven't seen his wonderful BBC documentary *Metro-Land* (1973), offering his own unique appreciation of suburbia, then you probably never will. So your life is poorer than it could be. At least make a point of seeing his statue if you're at St Pancras Station.

Betjeman was engaging, individualistic, amusing and different. He made you think and laugh. In 1983, a year before his death, when asked if he had any regrets, Betjeman mused for a while then replied, 'Yes, not enough sex.' After his death it emerged that he had done rather well on that front.

> Come, friendly bombs, and fall on Slough!
> It isn't fit for humans now.
> There isn't grass to graze a cow.
> Swarm over, Death!
> *'Slough', in* Continual Dew *(1937). At the time, Slough*
> *Trading Estate was expanding rapidly.*

Races won: none so far, and Betjeman isn't looking promising, but there's still time, possibly.

JOHN BETJEMAN (2016)
• Poet's Voice • A Great Beauty (Acclamation)

Maybe Betjeman was just a warm-up for John Betjeman. It's early days yet – always a good thing, because it means that hope hasn't died. So far, the two-year-old has run three times and lost three times.

METROLAND (2006)
• Royal Applause • Chetwynd (Exit To Nowhere)

Won twice, in 2008, doubtless as a tribute to the great man.

GK CHESTERTON (2013)
• Poet's Voice • Neptune's Bride (Bering)

Like TS Eliot, AA Milne, LP Hartley, PG Wodehouse and PD James, GK Chesterton (1874–1936) pleased quiz compilers by being known by his initials. The answer to the quiz question is Gilbert Keith. You can discover the others for yourself.

Chesterton spent a lot of his life agonising over whether to be an Anglican or a Catholic. In the end he opted for Catholicism. While agonising he did an enormous amount of writing and talking. He even had his own magazine, *GK's Weekly*, but is best known for his Father Brown short stories.

The only work of Chesterton's I've read is *The Man Who Was Thursday* (1908). It's a good title and if I could find my memory I'd tell you what I thought of it.

Surprisingly, given his size – Chesterton was very large both vertically and horizontally – he made a good racehorse. I'm glad, because it means that I can include the following:

George Bernard Shaw (thin): 'If I were as fat as you, I'd hang myself.'
GK Chesterton (fat): 'And if I had it in mind to hang myself, I'd use you as the rope.'

'Just the other day on the Underground I enjoyed the pleasure of offering my seat to three ladies.
GK Chesterton on one advantage of being large.

A lady confronting Chesterton during the First World War: 'Why are you not out at the front?'

GK Chesterton: 'My dear madam, if you will step round this way a little, you will see that I am.'

Races won: so far has won three times for Godolphin, including a valuable handicap at Epsom on Oaks Day in 2017.

CURBYOURENTHUSIASM (2011)
● Mastercraftsman ● Mohican Princess (Shirley Heights)

Exactly 18 letters – well done. It means that Larry David's great comedy series, starring Larry David, has celebrated its triumphs at Windsor, Doncaster and Chelmsford racecourses as well as on television.

If you haven't seen *Curb Your Enthusiasm* (2000–11, 2017 to date) then you're lucky, because you've got at least one thing to look forward to in life. The humour may not be to your taste, in which case you've got poor taste and are to be pitied.

Races won: won four times between 2013 and 2018.

---

400 NOCTE (1975)
● Royal Buck ● Beatrix (Escart III)

Racehorses aren't allowed to have names which include figures. The appearance of 400 Nocte in a hurdle race at Sandown in 1980, at the start of a racing career with trainer Nicky Henderson that lasted until 1984, appears to have triggered a change in the Rules.

It certainly posed a puzzle for the compilers of the Form Book, who chose to ignore the 400 and position 400 Nocte in the index where plain Nocte would have appeared. Timeform, on the other hand, treated him as an 'F'.

400 Nocte ran in the colours of Dr Roger Brimblecombe, a member of a team of researchers at what was then Smith Kline & French, an American company that had UK laboratories in Welwyn Garden City.

After a dozen years of research, the team developed a groundbreaking anti-ulcer drug based on cimetidine, which was launched in 1976 under the name Tagamet. 400 Nocte stands for a nightly dose of 400 mg.

Tagamet was enormously successful, with over a million patients treated in the UK within the first five years, and worldwide sales totalling over £150 million (equal to £1.2 billion today) in the first two years. The drug transformed the fortunes of Smith Kline & French, which went on to merge with Beecham. In 2000 SmithKline Beecham merged with Glaxo Wellcome to form GlaxoSmithKline.

Brimblecombe subsequently had a distinguished career, occupying many elevated posts in the pharmaceutical industry. 400 Nocte did rather less well and was sold in 1984.

'The pharmacology of cimetidine, a new histamine H2-receptor antagonist'
Brimblecombe, RW, et al, British Journal of Pharmacology, *March 1975*

Races won: one chase each year in 1981, 1982 and 1983.

HANCOCK'S HALF HOUR (1980)
• Comedy Star • Coaster (Right Tack)

Sadly, the owner of Hancock's Half Hour must have got far more pleasure from the classic comedy show than from the racehorse, who died after making just two appearances.

Between 1954 and 1961 *Hancock's Half Hour* managed far more, on both radio and television. In 1955 Harry Secombe stood in for Tony

Hancock for three episodes while Hancock was ill. One of the episodes was 'The Racehorse'. No recording of it has survived but the script has and was re-recorded and broadcast on BBC Radio 4 in 2017 as part of *The Missing Hancocks* series.

Bill Kerr buys a racehorse, to be trained by Sid James.

> **Bill:** 'There you are. It'd take a keen eye to find out why
> I only paid seven and six for that horse.'
> **Harry:** 'It's only got three legs.'
> **Bill:** 'Huh? Where, let me see ... one, two, three ... I've been
> cheated! So that's why he had it standing up against that post.'

Later, when Bill reveals that the horse, Sabrina, will be trained by Sid James ...

> **Harry:** 'That man's been warned off every racetrack
> in the country!'
> **Bill:** 'Only under one of his names.'

Races won: none.

QUINLAN TERRY (1985)
• Welsh Pageant • Quaranta (Hotfoot)

Quinlan Terry is a highly lauded architect and founder of a practice responsible, among many other projects, for designing the Maitland Robinson Library at Downing College, Cambridge University, restructuring Brentwood Cathedral and redesigning the interior of 10 Downing Street. Terry didn't design the equine swimming pool at Sir Mark Prescott's Heath House yard in Newmarket, but he helped to pay for it.

He did it by finishing in front of 28 other horses to win the 1988 Cambridgeshire Handicap at 11-1, although the horse's intimate connections doubtless backed the three-year-old at more lucrative odds.

The horse was bred and owned by Lord and Lady Fairhaven. When the race was won, Lord Fairhaven was the Jockey Club's senior steward and both he and his wife were keen on shooting, a fact possibly prominent in the mind of jockey George Duffield.

Remarkably, Prescott went on to win the Cambridgeshire twice more, with Pasternak in 1997, when stablemate Rudimental was runner-up, and with Chivalry in 2003.

Pasternak, owned by Graham Rock, the founding editor of the *Racing Post* and a close friend of Prescott, landed a huge public gamble. On the day of the Cambridgeshire Pasternak was backed from 11-1 to 4-1 favourite to beat 35 rivals, and did.

> Our greatest living architect... Terry's architecture
> is one large breath of fresh air.
> *Roger Scruton, 'Hail Quinlan Terry', in* The Spectator
> *8 April 2006*

Races won: four in 1988 and 1989. Three were minor affairs, the other wasn't.

A jolly good name

Miller's Tale (1982)
• *Mill Reef* • *Canterbury Tale (Exbury)*
'The Miller's Tale' was a bawdy story related by a drunken miller in Geoffrey Chaucer's fourteenth-century *Canterbury Tales*. As a racehorse, Miller's Tale won three times, the least a son of the Derby winner Mill Reef should do.

SAMUEL PEPYS (1971)
• Straight Lad • Panniers Premier (Pannier)

A civil servant and diarist rather than an athlete, Samuel Pepys (1633–1703) nevertheless made a fair fist of a radical change of career.

In his first incarnation, Pepys was a distinguished naval administrator, Chief Secretary to the Admiralty as well as an MP. His famous, and famously frank, diary covered only ten years, from 1660 to 1669, but is a unique source for a period that embraced the restoration of the monarchy under Charles II, the Great Plague of 1665 and the Great Fire of London the following year.

> To Sir William Batten's and there Mrs Knipp [Elizabeth Knipp or Knepp, an actress, singer and dancer] coming we did spend the evening together very merry. She and I singing and, God forgive me! I do still see that my nature is not to be quite conquered but will esteem pleasure above all things. Musique and women I cannot but give way to, whatever my business is.
> The Diary of Samuel Pepys, *9 March 1666*

Races won: after winning three hurdle races in Ireland in 1976, Samuel Pepys moved to England and won another hurdle and five chases, the last in 1981.

STEP ON DEGAS (1993)
* Superpower • Vivid Impression (Cure The Blues)

A splendid name and if the horse had been asked to paint instead of race he might have emulated Edgar Degas (1834–1917), the Impressionist who produced wonderful paintings and sculptures of ballet dancers and also of racecourse scenes.

One of the differences between *Step On Degas* and the artist – apart from one being a female horse and the other a male person – was that the former cost less than 3,000 guineas, whereas the latter's work now tends to cost rather more. In 2008, Degas's *Danseuse au repos* fetched $37 million (£25 million). It's not even that big.

Paul Mellon (if you read the bit about *Wait For The Will*, which is after the bit about Arkle, which is near the beginning, he's mentioned there) donated a major collection of Degas's work to the National Gallery of Art in Washington DC.

Damn, and just when I was starting to get it.
Degas on his deathbed

Races won: four out of 57 between 1995 and 2001.

AMEDEO MODIGLIANI (2015)
• Galileo • Gooseberry Fool (Danehill Dancer)

Amedeo Modigliani was regularly short of paint so often gave his figures thin faces. They are captivating, if repetitive. Still, if you like something, repetition is welcome. It's the same with cashew nuts.

Modigliani (1884–1920) packed a lot of painting, drawing, sculpting and women into his short life, mainly in Paris, and he didn't do badly when Coolmore converted him into a racehorse, initially as *Modigliani (1998) Danzig – Hot Princess (Hot Spark)*. Yet despite winning twice, including the 2001 Group 3 Tetrarch Stakes, the equine Modigliani became unfashionable and in 2012 passed unsold through Keeneland's sales ring at just $19,000.

Undeterred, John Magnier's team named a 750,000 guineas purchase Amedeo Modigliani. The colt looked promising when winning a maiden race in 2017 but not as promising as the Modigliani that Magnier had bought for $26.9 million (then £16.7 million) in 2003. In 2018 the painting, *Nu Couché (sur le côté gauche)* was sold at Sotheby's for $157.2 million (£117 million). She didn't even have any clothes on.

With one eye you are looking at the outside world while with the other you are looking within yourself.
Amedeo Modigliani

Races won: just the one so far.

TAXIDERMIST (1952)
• Ujiji • Rage Bleue (Plassy)

A horse crying out to get stuffed, yet in 1958 he won both the Whitbread Gold Cup and Hennessy Gold Cup when trained by Fulke Walwyn and ridden by the accomplished amateur rider John Lawrence, later Lord Oaksey.

Having been bought for £400 as a three-year-old, Taxidermist went on to win once on the Flat and a dozen times over fences. The Grand National proved a fence too big – Taxidermist fell in 1961 and was pulled up a year later. It was brave of him to try.

I ask people why they have deer heads on their walls. They always say, 'Because it's such a beautiful animal.' There you go. I think my mother is attractive, but I have photographs of her. *Ellen DeGeneres, comedian*

Maybe I'll learn a trade. I've considered taxidermy. I always thought it was a shame you couldn't do that on people. *The wonderfully funny David Sedaris (1956 to it's too soon to say)*

THE GO-BETWEEN (1970)
• Runnymede • Game Girl (Abernant)

LP Hartley's haunting novel, published in 1953, was turned into a fine film in 1971. With a screenplay written by Harold Pinter and a star-filled cast, *The Go-Between* garnered a string of awards. If you were male and aged 22, your award went to Julie Christie.

The Go-Between must have made an impression on trainer Jeremy Hindley and owner Mrs D. Helmann because in 1972 The Go-Between turned up as a horse and swept most before him, winning eight of his 11 races. Timeform's *Racehorses of 1972* described him as 'the fastest two-year-old colt of the year'. As a three-year-old The Go-Between won only once but was a creditable third in the Nunthorpe Stakes.

The past is a foreign country. They do things differently there.
The memorable opening line of LP Hartley's The Go-Between

Races won: nine, including the 1972 Group 3 Cornwallis Stakes.

A classical name, in its way

Brahms And Liszt (1976)
• *Will Somers* • *Fancy Pants (Galivanter)*
A cockney tribute to two celebrated composers. Brahms And Liszt won
once on the Flat, in 1979, and from a huge number of races over jumps
won two hurdle races, in 1979 and 1981, and one chase, in 1983.

WILFRED OWEN (2015)
• *Poet's Voice* • *Mini Mosa (Indian Ridge)*

Wilfred Owen's final, piercing salvo of First World War poems,
written in his early 20s, left an enduring impression. C. Day Lewis,
in his introduction to *The Collected Poems of Wilfred Owen* (1963),
judged them, as many did, to be 'the finest written by any English
poet of the First War'. Owen's death was as poignant as his poems,
for he was killed on the Western Front in November 1918, a week
before the Armistice was signed.

> What passing-bells for these who die as cattle?
> Only the monstrous anger of the guns.
> Only the stuttering rifles' rapid rattle
> Can patter out their hasty orisons.
> No mockeries now for them; no prayers nor bells,
> Nor any voice of mourning save the choirs, –
> The shrill, demented choirs of wailing shells;
> And bugles calling for them from sad shires.
> *From Wilfred Owen,* 'Anthem For Doomed Youth' *(1917)*

Races won: none, but there's still time.

14. ANIMAL, VEGETABLE, MINERAL

ANIMAL

ALLIGATOR (2014)
• Sepoy • See You Later (Emarati)

Initially owned, appropriately, by the Ciao For Now Syndicate, Alligator may have done better in a river race. Being a racehorse just didn't suit him.

> See you later alligator, after 'while crocodile,
> See you later alligator, after 'while crocodile.
> Can't you see you're in my way now,
> Don't you know you cramp my style.
> *Bill Haley and His Comets, 'See You Later, Alligator' (1956)*

Races won: sadly, none so far, from 14 tries between 2016 and 2018.

RED ALLIGATOR (1959)
• Magic Red • Miss Alligator (Hyacinthus)

Given Red Alligator's sire and dam, his name wasn't surprising.

Unless I've added up wrongly, Red Alligator won one hurdle and 12 chases between 1964 and 1970. Having finished third in the 1967 Grand National he won the great race in 1968, when trained by Denys Smith and ridden by Brian Fletcher.

More interesting is the fact that 14 places behind Red Alligator was Highlandie, ridden by Mr Tim Durant, a 68-year-old American.

Durant was an accomplished baseball and tennis player who made a lot of money as a New York stockbroker, then lost it in the 1929 Wall Street Crash.

Two years earlier he had married Adelaide Post, the daughter of the extremely wealthy Marjorie Post. By the time Durant moved to Hollywood, in 1936, he had plenty of money but no wife. This left him free to dally with actresses such as Joan Fontaine, Paulette Goddard and Olivia de Havilland, as well as befriend Charlie Chaplin, John Huston, José Ferrer and Ronald Reagan. When the West Hills Hunt Club staged a steeplechase in 1951, Reagan and Durant were both among the officials. Durant was a past President of the United Hunts Racing Association.

His friendship with Chaplin, Huston and Ferrer helped get him parts, mainly small ones, in *The Red Badge of Courage* (1951), *Limelight* (1952), *The List of Adrian Messenger* (1963) and *Return to Peyton Place* (1961).

By the late 1950s Durant had decided that he'd like to ride in the Grand National. Interesting, isn't it?

> It's much easier to teach riders to act than it is to teach actors to ride.
> *John Huston, offering encouragement to Tim Durant before casting him as the General in* The Red Badge of Courage.

A fine name

Sizzling Melody (1984)
• Song • Mrs Bacon (Balliol)
A sizzler he was. As a two-year-old, Sizzling Melody won the Group 2 Flying Childers Stakes and Group 3 Norfolk Stakes. The following year he won the Group 3 Prix du Petit Couvert. Over the two seasons that he raced, Sizzling Melody won six out of 12 races. Well done.

RHODE ISLAND RED (1983)
• Henbit • Embarrassed (Busted)

An embarrassed, red-faced hen? Can chickens feel embarrassed? Probably not, and the Rhode Island Red has every right to feel proud. It's exotic, being the product of nineteenth-century matings between Oriental and Italian breeds, it's colourful, the hens are terrific at laying eggs and, not least, it's the State bird of Rhode Island.

In 1954 Rhode Island held an election to decide which bird would represent the State. There were five candidates and the Rhode Island Red won the election. Governor Dennis Roberts signed the Bill that gave the Rhode Island Red legal standing.

It was a cracking year for Rhode Island because it also marked the launch of the Newport Jazz Festival. Duke Ellington, Ray Charles, Dionne Warwick, Nina Simone and more. Yes, that Rhode Island Red is some bird. Even as a horse, there have been a lot worse.

The Rhode Island Red has become a symbol of Rhode Islanders all over the world.
Governor Roberts on signing the Bill making the chicken the State's official bird, 3 May 1954.

Races won: six times over jumps between 1987 and 1992.

FIGHTING COCK (1972)
• Aggressor • Rhode Island (Pardal)

Won a hurdle in 1975 and two chases, in 1978 and 1981.

Sir Cumference (1996)
* *Sir Harry Lewis* • *Puki Puki (Roselier)*
Won three chases in 2003 and 2005.

SPAGHETTI MOUSE (2002)
* Archers Bay • Desert Mouse (With Approval)

In 1955 Nick and Pauline Felicella opened a coffee shop at 631 Commercial Drive in Vancouver. It became Nick's Spaghetti House and racegoers from the nearby Hastings racetrack were regular customers.

As the business prospered, in 1979 the couple bought their first racehorse, called Fire Ball. A lot of other horses followed and the walls of Nick's Spaghetti House became covered with photographs of the winners. Then there was Spaghetti Mouse.

The Felicellas bought him as a yearling for $18,000. Between 2004 and 2012, Spaghetti Mouse ran 52 times, every time at Hastings, where he became the race fans' favourite. He won a dozen races and $929,850, a record for a horse bred in British Columbia.

At the end of 2017, the Felicellas finally gave up their Spaghetti House and retired to their ranch, but they still own racehorses.

> After the races all the jockeys, trainers and grooms would come down and have dinner and drinks. They were good-time people, spent lots of money, and were always talking horses.
> *Nick Felicella, recalling how he became interested in racing*

> There's never going to be a restaurant in Vancouver like Nick's. I'm just going to miss everything about it.
> *Susan MacDonald, who worked there, 2017*

TEQUILAMOCKINGBIRD (1987)
• Far Out East • Little Miss Misty (Misty Day)

... and

TEQUILAMOCKINGBIRD (2010)
• Bold Executive • Domasca Bella (Domasca Dan)

Neither had pedigrees pointing towards Tequilamockingbird but I like the name. Harper Lee wrote the classic novel *To Kill a Mockingbird* in 1960 and Gregory Peck starred in the 1962 film, also a classic. You probably already knew that.

You may not know that Peck became interested in horseracing through working with film director John Huston on *Moby Dick* (1956). They had horses together and Peck later owned several himself, including Owen's Sedge, who won the 1963 Leopardstown Chase and finished seventh in that year's Grand National. Two years earlier, when asked what he liked about filming in England, Peck replied, 'What do I do in England? Racehorses are my passion, a passion shared by the British.'

In 1966, Different Class rounded off an excellent season by winning the Totalisator Champion Novices' Chase (now the RSA Chase) at the Cheltenham Festival in Peck's colours. He returned a year later and won the National Hunt Handicap Chase, before heading to Aintree for the Grand National. It was the year of Foinavon. Different Class was brought down. He was back again in 1968 and, sent off as favourite, finished third to Red Alligator.

Gregory Peck retained his passion for the Grand National and was there in 1997, on his 81st birthday, when a bomb threat caused the race to be postponed for two days.

> I think it will be a great pity if the Grand National was discontinued. In my opinion it is the greatest sporting event in the world.
> *Gregory Peck, speaking on the eve of the 1967 National*

Races won: the 1987 Tequilamockingbird won 15 times from 93 runs between 1989 and 1995 but earned a derisory $33,632. That's because he was winning in New Mexico. The 2010 version won three times from ten runs but earned $118,951. She was racing at Woodbine.

ATTICUS FINCH

Named, several times, after the main character in *To Kill a Mockingbird*, the heroic lawyer played by Gregory Peck.

There are so many Atticus Finches, I just can't face them all.

> Shoot all the blue jays you want, if you can hit 'em, but remember it's a sin to kill a mockingbird.
> *Atticus Finch in* To Kill a Mockingbird *(1962)*

THE DRUNKEN DUCK (1973)
• Pony Express • Polly Buckle (Polic)

For those alive at the time (1982) and still alive now (2018, so there's no guarantee), The Drunken Duck's victory in the Foxhunter Chase at the Cheltenham Festival was memorable. Not so much for the horse as for its rider, Mr Broderick Munro-Wilson.

The Drunken Duck was named after an inn near Ambleside, in the Lake District. The inn was named after an unlikely incident in the nineteenth century when the landlady discovered a collection of apparently dead ducks and prepared them for the oven, only to discover that they were merely dead drunk, having sipped the contents of a leaking beer barrel. Instead of cooking them, the landlady knitted waistcoats for the ducks while their plucked feathers grew back.

What Munro-Wilson offered in energy and enthusiasm he lacked in style. He had a style but it was reminiscent of a bygone age. The posture was verging on the vertical, the stirrups were long and, in a finish, the body and arms hyperactive. Among racegoers, horse and rider attracted a following. Among other triumphs, they were rewarded by the sight of victory for the partnership in the 1981 Grand Military Gold Cup at Sandown, a race Munro-Wilson had won the previous year on Beeno.

Munro-Wilson was not short of courage. His first success under Rules, on Champers Galore at Plumpton in 1975, was achieved despite riding with his wrist in plaster after breaking it at a recent point-to-point meeting. In 1980 he rode Coolishall in the Grand National. Unfortunately his stirrups broke and he was unseated.

Later, Munro-Wilson had similarly mixed fortunes in various court proceedings. In 1993 he was famously rebuked by Mr Justice Otton, who remarked, in relation to Munro-Wilson's behaviour towards a former girlfriend, 'I would expect you to behave like a gentleman and not a cad.'

> I like to ride like a gentleman, not a monkey on a stick, which is why I rarely take a tumble. Length of leg, that's what it's all about!
> *Broderick Munro-Wilson*

Races won: The Drunken Duck won six times under Rules between 1981 and 1985, on four occasions ridden by Munro-Wilson.

Just names

No Speed No Feed (2002)
* *Bankbook* • *No Pay No Hay (Consul General)*
From 28 tries, won once, at Charles Town in West Virginia in 2005.

Ima Reel Bimbo (2001)
* *Reel On Reel* • *I'm No Bimbo (Hold Your Peace)*
Raced in Nebraska, where there isn't much racing nowadays, Ima Reel Bimbo won three times, including at Fonner Park and Atokad. Never heard of them.

THE GREEN MONKEY (2004)
● Forestry ● Magical Masquerade (Unbridled)

Rivalry between the mega-rich can get silly. Take the sale of an unraced two-year-old colt at Calder in Florida on 28 February 2006. Seven months earlier, Randy Hartley and Dean De Renzo had bought the colt for $425,000. On 19 February they breezed him at Calder over one furlong. The colt covered the eighth of a mile in a spectacularly fast 9.8 seconds.

A circumspect adviser might have pointed out that there aren't any races over one furlong but speed appeals and the colt appealed to two men whose relationship had soured – Sheikh Mohammed and John Magnier, two of the big beasts of racing.

Sheikh Mohammed sent John Ferguson to bid for him, while Magnier sent Demi O'Byrne. Commercial calculations quickly became secondary to a determination to win. With the law of diminishing returns ejected from the building, O'Byrne made the final $16 million (at that time the equivalent of £9.2 million) bid, the highest ever at a public auction. 'He'd better be good,' O'Byrne remarked.

Coolmore's newcomer was named after the currently $390-a-round golf course attached to Magnier and friends' luxury Sandy Lane resort in Barbados, the Green Monkey. Sent to trainer Todd Pletcher, The Green Monkey was injured and didn't race until September 2007. After three failures, he was retired to stud with earnings of $10,440.

Standing at a fee of just $5,000, The Green Monkey failed to hit the heights as a stallion, his best offspring the filly Kinz Funky Monkey, winner at Hollywood Park in 2013. The Green Monkey died in 2018.

A very nice-looking horse. A pity he didn't show his potential.
Alfredo Lichoa, stallion manager at Hartley/De Renzo
Thoroughbreds at Ocala, Florida

Races won: none.

Hedge Warbler (1970)
* *Sing Sing* • *Wind Break (Borealis)*
Won twice in 1972 and 1973.

VEGETABLE

CABBAGE (1921)
* Adular • Colewort (Colin)

It's not unusual for a Cabbage to turn into a racehorse. They seem to find it quite easy.

This equine Cabbage was offered for sale almost as often as the vegetable. In 1923 he won selling races at Lincoln, Wolverhampton and Epsom, as well as a non-seller at Yarmouth. In 1925 he won a seller at Nottingham and in 1926 sellers at Chester and Epsom. Maybe his owners weren't very fond of Cabbage. In 2005, in the USA, a rather poor *Cabbage (1999)* put up three rotten displays at Penn National. Ten years later, another *Cabbage (2011)* managed to win two small races at Fresno and Golden Gate in California.

On the other side of the globe, a Tom Mulholland-trained *Cabbage (2001)* won twice at New South Wales tracks in 2009.

The best Cabbage of all was *Spring Cabbage (1963)*. Highly prized at Harry Blackshaw's Middleham yard, Spring Cabbage bolted up 15 times in the 1960s.

I expect another one will be on the market soon.

> Spring cabbage: Sow in July/August; transplant
> in September/October.
> *Royal Horticultural Society,* How To Grow Cabbages

Doughnut (1969)

• *Crepes d'Enfer* • *Jeopardy (Grey Sovereign)*

Of course he was hopeless – too fat.

CAULIFLOWER (1895)

• Common • Ethel Agnes (Bend Or)

Strange to think that in the 1890s Mr Fairie looked at his filly and thought, 'She's got Cauliflower written all over her.' Then he named her after a very slow vegetable although, admittedly, no slower than other vegetables.

It didn't prevent Cauliflower from finishing third in the 1898 Oaks and fourth in that year's Coronation Stakes but may explain why, subsequently, she went off.

> Explaining something sensible to Lord Killanin is akin to explaining something to a cauliflower. The advantage of the cauliflower is that, if all else fails, you can always cover it with melted cheese and eat it.
> *William E. Simon, Secretary of the US Treasury, 1974 to 1977, in an article in the* New York Times, *29 July 1984. Lord Killanin was a former President of the International Olympic Committee, of which Simon was a member, and a prominent figure in Irish racing. Others thought much more highly of him.*

Gangrene (2002)

• *Bates Motel* • *Momento's Lady (Momento)*

Gangrene! Unbelievable. No wonder she failed to win in 21 attempts.

CWRW (1809)
• Dick Andrews • Lady Charlotte (Buzzard)

The winner of the 1812 2,000 Guineas seems to be missing a vowel. Not in Wales, however, where the word means beer.

That was the least of Cwrw's oddities. Making his racecourse debut in the 2,000 Guineas, Cwrw was assumed to be his owner Lord Darlington's second string, behind a colt by Remembrancer.

There were good grounds for this belief. First, the Remembrancer colt had been heavily backed and, second, he was ridden to the post by the well-known jockey Sam Chifney, whereas his stablemate was ridden there by a stable groom.

When they reached the post, Chifney swopped mounts, the Remembrancer colt was withdrawn and, when Cwrw won, Lord Darlington and his associates landed a memorable gamble. Under the existing rules, bets on the non-runner were declared void.

Admiral Rous, a leading figure in Turf administration in the nineteenth century, cited the case in his book, *On the Laws and Practice of Horse-Racing* (1850), as a reason for changing the rules on betting.

> His first and chief ambition was to shine as a sportsman.
> He spared no expense in the splendour of his kennels
> and stables.
> *Obituary of Lord Darlington (later the Duke of Cleveland)*
> *in* The Gentleman's Magazine, *May 1842*

Races won: six, but the 1812 2,000 Guineas was the one that mattered.

HARICOT (1870)
• Ladykirk • Saucepan (Colsterdale)

Baked beans are wonderful things. Whether you eat them hot or cold, they are quick and easy to prepare (especially if cold). So it's no great surprise that Haricot shone in the 1874 Melbourne Cup, although it came as a surprise to most race fans and punters, who sent Haricot off at 15-1.

The reporter for Melbourne's main newspaper, the *Argus*, was unimpressed by the great day. The Melbourne Cup was not yet the race that stops a nation but in 1873 it became the race that stopped part of a nation when the Governor of Victoria, Sir George Ferguson Bowen, proclaimed the day of the race to be a 'special day to be observed as a Bank Holiday throughout Victoria'.

The *Argus* considered the 1874 edition, with a crowd estimated at anything from 20,000 to 80,000, not special enough. 'The sport was of a very inferior description,' their correspondent complained, 'there not being a good finish during the day.'

He was not impressed by Haricot's appearance. 'Haricot's style when going slowly is not at all taking, and few that saw the peacocky gentleman dancing along the green sward thought he would be able to lead such a field in the two-mile race.' The reporter was mistaken. Carrying only 6st 7lb, Haricot set up a clear lead under jockey Paddy Piggott and was never caught.

The arrangements for comfort were generally considered to be execrable. The crush was terrible. The racing itself was as bad as could be. Before they had gone a mile Haricot came through his horses like a bullet through a cornfield and at the abattoirs he was leading by fifty lengths. From that moment there was not a question as to his victory. The ringmen embraced, the public cursed and the jockey weighed in amid something very like hissing.

Brisbane Courier, *25 November 1874*

HORLICKS (1983)
• Three Legs • Malt (Moss Trooper)

The thing to do with Horlicks is to eat it. Not every day but now and again, when the mood takes you. Quite quickly it sticks to the spoon but I think you'll find it's worth it. Or you can make a drink from it, or a horse.

The best one, a terrific grey mare bred and trained in New Zealand, did the opposite of making a horlicks of things. She was a champion. (I suppose she should be in the Champions chapter but now she's here she might as well stay).

Races won: won 17 times, including five Group 1 races in New Zealand and Australia. Capped her career by winning the 1989 Japan Cup. Fantastic.

A bubbly name

Dom Perignon (1975)
* *Sparkler* • *Breathalyser (Alcide)*
Won three times on the Flat between 1978 and 1980.

PARSNIP (2014)
* *Zebedee* • *Hawattef (Mujtahid)*

Who knows why? Lady Bamford, probably, as she bought Parsnip and probably sells parsnips in her Daylesford organic shops.

This was a particularly expensive Parsnip, costing 280,000 guineas as a yearling. After winning once from four tries in 2016, at the end of 2017 Parsnip was sold for 160,000 guineas. Maybe she'll breed more Parsnips.

Smelly names

Judge Smells (1983)
• *In Reality* • *Timeforaturn (Best Turn)*
He might smell but he won all three races he contested, including the 1985 Grade 3 Hollywood Prevue Stakes at Hollywood Park. After that, perhaps he was overcome by his own fumes.

Odor In The Court (1996)
• *Judge Smells* • *Faffy G (Capital Idea)*
Maybe not as smelly as his father, won two small races in New Jersey in 1999 and 2000.

POTOOOOOOOO (1773)
• *Eclipse* • *Sports Mistress (Regulus)*

During the 1770s the eccentric 4th Earl of Abingdon decided to call a horse Potatoes. In 1827 the popular but perhaps apocryphal explanation reached the pages of the *Sheffield Independent*.

> His Majesty [King George IV] has made known in the sporting world that the Earl of Abingdon named his celebrated horse Pot8os from the following circumstance.
> His Lordship intended to call him Potatoes and he was in fact so named. One day his Lordship asked one of his stable boys if he could spell the name of the animal in question, with the promise of a guinea if he succeeded. The boy wrote upon the stall with chalk, Potooooooooo, which pleased the Earl, who determined that the horse should retain the name written by the boy.

During the horse's early racing career the son of Eclipse did run under the name of Potooooooooo and later under that of Pot8os. In 1778, Potooooooooo ran in the prestigious 1,200 Guineas. During the course of the race, the Earl of Abingdon agreed to sell the horse to Lord Grosvenor for 1,500 guineas, with Grosvenor taking the prize money if Potoooooooo won. He did win. Grosvenor later remarked, 'The boy could count, even if he couldn't spell.'

> Methought I saw all studs surrender,
> Beat by Potooooooooo or Pretender.
> *4th Earl of Abingdon*, An Adieu to the Turf *(1778).*
> *Pretender was a prolific winner for Abingdon.*

Races won: 1778 1,200 Guineas, plus at least 27 other races between 1777 and 1782.

Bizarre names

My Ex Wifes Ashes (1999)
• *Islefaxyou* • *Duck Decoy (Quack)*
Possibly not named out of affection. Won a race at Penn National in 2003.

Olivia Loves Jesus (1998)
• *Launch A Leader* • *Fuzzy Halo (Fuzzy)*
It didn't help, because she ran 27 times between 2001 and 2003 without success.

Tom Likes Beetroot (2004)
• *Snaadee* • *Hesyan (Secret Savings)*
That didn't help either. Racing in Australia, Tom liking beetroot was to no avail in 13 races in 2008 and 2009.

WALDORF SALAD (2008)
• Millenary • Ismene (Bad Conduct)

Owner-breeder Alan Parker must be a fan of *Fawlty Towers* and, in particular, of the wonderful episode in which Harry Hamilton, a brash American guest, orders a Waldorf salad. The salad, based on apples, celery, grapes and toasted walnuts, was first served at the Waldorf Astoria Hotel in New York in 1896. Its fame had not reached the Fawlty Towers Hotel in Torquay, resulting in some memorable exchanges.

As a horse, Waldorf Salad was less disastrous, winning five jumps races between 2012 and 2018.

> **Mr Hamilton:** 'Could you make me a Waldorf salad?'
> **Basil Fawlty:** 'Waldorf salad. I think we're just out of Waldorfs.'
> Fawlty Towers, *'Waldorf Salad' (1979)*

Races won: I've already told you.

SALAD (1974)
• New Member • Bonny Legend (Border Legend)

Despite his light diet, won four hurdles and two chases between 1979 and 1984.

MINERAL

PHOSPHORUS (1870)
• Lamplighter • Rubens mare (Rubens)

At school, phosphorus brought chemistry lessons to life. Everyone perked up at the sight of a sample of the element going up in flames, with the exciting prospect that the school might follow its example.

Maybe the 9th Baron Berners had a similar experience in mind when naming his home-bred colt Phosphorus. Like the mineral, Phosphorus burned brightly but briefly. Regularly lame, he ran only three times in England, the final time being in the 1837 Derby.

Bell's Life and Sporting Chronicle reported that one Derby Day racegoer said, dismissively, 'Phosphorus has not the ghost of a hope and has scarce fire enough to light a cigar.' In the previous week's edition, 'Vates' stood alone in tipping the 40-1 outsider.

It was an inspired selection and Phosphorus's victory was greeted with disbelief. The following February 'Craven' in the *Sporting Magazine* was still bemused. He wondered, 'How could Phosphorus, a weak-looking little cripple, beat the field he met for last year's Derby?'

Lord Berners died in March 1838, and Phosphorus was bought by the Duke of Brunswick for 1,000 guineas and sent to Germany. Chronically unsound, he never won again.

> 'Tis over – the trick for the thousands is done,
> George Edwards on Phosphorus the Derby has won!
> *'Vates', in a very long poem titled 'The Prophecy – The Derby*
> *for 1837' in* Bell's Life and Sporting Chronicle, *21 May 1837*

SODIUM (1963)
• Psidium • Gambade (Big Game)

Usually associated with salt which, according to my grandmother, was to be avoided because 'it dries up your blood'. Maybe that's why they stopped putting those nice blue salt sachets in packets of crisps. Evidently salt raises your blood pressure, so watching a close finish while eating salted peanuts could be fatal.

As a horse, Sodium won the 1966 Irish Derby and St Leger. That wasn't much use to Jeffrey Bernard, who borrowed £100 to back Charlottown in the Epsom Derby, then changed his mind and backed Sodium instead. Charlottown won.

You can have an entertaining time finding out more about Bernard in Graham Lord's *Just The One: The Wives and Times of Jeffrey Bernard* (1992).

I never travel. I went abroad once to a place called Passchendaele, didn't like it, have never been abroad again.
Trainer George Todd, explaining why he wasn't at the Curragh to see Sodium win the Irish Derby

Races won: the two Classics I've already mentioned, plus the 1966 Derby Trial at Brighton. In those days they used to have races like that at Brighton. Those glory days have long gone but Brighton still stages the Ian Carnaby Selling Stakes, sponsored by the notable racing writer, so all isn't lost.

ZINC (1820)
* Woful * Zaida (Sir Peter Teazle)

When Zinc was born, in 1820, zinc was still a relatively novel mineral in Europe and the 4th Duke of Grafton, who bred and owned Zinc, was therefore a pioneer in the zinc industry.

Although he made no mark in politics or much else, the 4th Duke (1760–1844) enjoyed tremendous success on the Turf. When Zinc won the 1823 1,000 Guineas she was the fifth winner of the race in a row for him, with three more to come from 1825 to 1827. Zinc's Oaks win was one of six in that Classic registered by the sporting aristocrat, who also won the 2,000 Guineas five times, and the Derby. So much for Coolmore.

His grace deserves success, for he is a nobleman of high character on the Turf and unlike too many owners of racehorses we could name, always runs to win.
R. Darvill in American Turf Register and Sporting Magazine, *1838*

Races won: 1823 1,000 Guineas and Oaks and three other races.

15. POWER, POLITICS AND PHILOSOPHY

ALFRED THE GREAT (1933)
• King's Oven • Tyen (Craig an Eran)

Over a thousand years after Alfred the Great (849–99) was asked to look after some cakes baking by a fire, he was still being given a hard time for letting them burn.

Generations of schoolchildren were told the story of Alfred fleeing battle and taking refuge in a peasant woman's hovel, where he was asked to mind the cakes while she went out to milk a cow. When she got back the cakes had been burnt to death.

It was probably meant as a cautionary tale to let girls know what they could expect if they put their trust in a man. Well, if you'd had the Vikings chasing you across Somerset waving swords and axes you'd probably have more on your mind than teacakes. Anyway, when Alfred eventually defeated the Vikings I expect he visited the old lady and gave her an enormous Christmas cake. The history books conveniently ignore that.

Life was much easier for Alfred as a racehorse, with meals brought to him, if not on a plate, then in his stable.

Races won: none. He didn't race until he was five and clearly didn't think much of it when he did.

BOB MAXWELL (2014)
• Big Bad Bob • Catching Stars (Halling)

He was undeniably big, extremely bad and, from the 1940s, Bob, so I suppose former Tote chairman Peter Jones was entitled to name his horse Bob Maxwell.

Robert Maxwell was a particularly obnoxious, egocentric fraudster who fell off his yacht and drowned in 1991, having pillaged his companies' pension funds in an attempt to stave off the collapse of his empire.

After distinguished service in the Second World War, Maxwell, who was born Jan Ludvik Hoch in what was then Czechoslovakia, built up a large publishing business. From 1964 to 1970 he was also an unlikely Labour MP.

In 1969, concern over aspects of the proposed sale of Maxwell's Pergamon Press prompted an investigation by inspectors from the Department of Trade and Industry. Two years later their interim report was highly critical of Maxwell, who they felt had excessive confidence in his own ability and other, worse flaws. His reports to shareholders were deemed to show 'reckless and unjustified optimism' that led him 'to state what he must have known to be untrue'. The inspectors concluded that Maxwell was not 'a person who can be relied on to exercise proper stewardship of a publicly quoted company'. Two further reports, in 1972 and 1973, were similarly damning.

The notoriously litigious Maxwell failed in his legal challenges against the DTI but, sadly, was still able to pursue his business career. Through his later ownership of Mirror Group Newspapers, he owned *The Sporting Life*.

Very overweight, Bob Maxwell was unlikely to thrive at a racecourse, except on the downhill stretches.

Maxwell was a public danger. I felt we had to prevent him getting away. The report took two years to prepare

and was upheld at the High Court, but you would think
nobody read it.
Sir Ronald Leach, leader of the 1969 to 1971 investigation
by the DTI

Races won: none so far.

FREDERICK ENGELS (2009)
* Iceman * Colonel's Daughter (Colonel Collins)

Sidekick of Karl Marx (see below), owner of impressive beard
(see Karl Marx), joint-author of *The Communist Manifesto* (see Karl
Marx), sole author of *The Condition of the Working Class in England*
and enthusiastic fox hunter, Friedrich Engels (1820–95) anglicised
his name and became a horse in 2009.

A precocious child, as a two-year-old he won three races,
including the Windsor Castle Stakes at Royal Ascot and the
Group 2 July Stakes at Newmarket. By then Frederick Engels was
owned by Sheikh Fahad Al Thani of Qatar, who was not himself
a communist.

In 2012 Frederick Engels moved to Hong Kong, where he won
three races that year and, in 2013, twice finished runner-up in
local Group 1 events. Flourishing in a capitalist society, by the time
Frederick Engels retired, in 2016, he had earned HK$9.41 million
(£790,000).

On Saturday, I went out fox-hunting – seven hours in
the saddle. That sort of thing always keeps me in a state
of devilish excitement for several days; it's the greatest
physical pleasure I know.
Friedrich Engels to Karl Marx, 1857. Engels hunted regularly
with the Cheshire Hounds. It's a funny old world.

KARL MARX (2010)
• Red Clubs • Brillano (Desert King)

Famous for his impressive beard, appearances at the British Museum Reading Room and being buried in Highgate Cemetery, as well as for writing *The Communist Manifesto* and *Das Kapital*, Karl Marx (1818–83) was an unlikely enthusiast for horseracing.

Horseracing society was remote from the classless society envisaged by Marx and it was fitting that Karl Marx (equine division) was to be found in the working-class section of the race programme, among the humbler horses.

It took Karl Marx 21 goes before he arrived in the winner's enclosure, after a selling hurdle at Exeter in 2014, but after 48 more races he could boast a total of six wins, albeit at a humble level.

> From each according to his ability, to each according to his needs.
> *Karl Marx, 1875. The principle was applied to his equine namesake, who raced as well as he could and was given breakfast and dinner every day.*

A brain name

Mensa (1974)
• *High Top* • *Intelligentsia (Fortino II)*
Much too clever to run as hard as her riders wanted her to, and was therefore a non-winner. Mensa preferred to save her energy for solving puzzles in her stable.

LENIN (2015)
• Arakan • Virginia Woolf (Daylami)

It is not widely known that Lenin's mother was Virginia Woolf. Woolf (1882–1941) devoted herself to writing a string of revolutionary novels, while Lenin (1870–1924), having demonstrated his radical nature by being born before his mother, devoted himself to the overthrow of capitalism and establishment of a socialist society.

Virginia Woolf (2002) was the first to turn to horseracing, winning three times on the Flat and once over hurdles in Ireland between 2005 and 2007. Lenin waited until 2015 for his resurrection. By then Marxism-Leninism had lost its popularity and at the Sales in 2016 the young Lenin was valued at just €9,500. Two runs for trainer Stan Moore in 2017 failed to mark the centenary of the Bolshevik Revolution in a triumphant manner.

> As long as she thinks of a man, nobody objects
> to a woman thinking.
> *Virginia Woolf,* Orlando *(1928)*

> Capitalists are no more capable of self-sacrifice than a man
> is capable of lifting himself up by his own bootstraps.
> *Vladimir Lenin,* Letters from Afar *(1917)*

A communist

Red in Bed (2004)
• *Moscow Society* • *Secret Tryst (Roi Danzig)*
If she'd got out of bed she might have done better. As it was, she failed to score in three races under Rules and 15 point-to-points between 2008 and 2011.

DAME ELIZABETH ACKROYD

Dame Elizabeth Ackroyd, known by her critics as 'Queen of the Quangos', was a prolific founder and director of governmental and non-governmental organisations.

In 1963, while a civil servant at the Board of Trade, Ackroyd was appointed to be the first Director of the new Consumer Council.

From 1971 she was President of the Patients Association and made her name in the field of consumer protection.

Ackroyd (1910–87) amassed a remarkable collection of posts, including with the Eggs Authority, Pedestrians' Association, South Eastern Electricity Board, Metrication Board, Post Office Users' Council, West Roding Community Health Council, Council for the Securities Industry and Cinematograph Films Council.

In her spare time, if she had any, Dame Elizabeth enjoyed racing. In 1975 she became the first female member of the Tote Board and two years later chairman of the Bloodstock and Racehorse Industries Confederation, a powerless body set up to enable the Jockey Club to say that it was consulting professionals. In 1979 Ackroyd was elected to the Jockey Club.

Ackroyd had several horses in training with Hugh Collingridge but one stood out, not for his achievements but his name.

MORON (1975)
* Morston * One Extra (Abernant)

Not a good name for a horse, nor for a person.

> It is delightful to imagine a day in Dame Elizabeth's busy life of consumer research: an egg for breakfast, cooked by electricity, a walk to the post office on the way to the hospital in West Roding, a flutter on the Tote, and a film in the evening; a consumer's work is never done.
> *Anthony Sampson attacking quangos in the* Observer,
> *23 September 1979*

Races won: four, all in 1979.

Vaguely related names

Beggars Belief (1996)
• *Common Grounds* • *Perfect Alibi (Law Society)*
An apt comment on the previous name. Won twice in 1999.

Dim Wit (1965)
• *Star Signal* • *Miss Wise (Old Radnor)*
Not a very nice thing to call a horse, is it? There were children a lot dimmer at my school.

Despite the insult, Dim Wit did owner Jeremiah J. O'Neill, trainer Paddy Mullins and jockey Matt Curran proud, winning the 1972 Irish Grand National as well as ten other races.

GENERAL GORDON (2000)
• Washington State • Mossalier (Mazilier)

Given how awry things went for General Charles George Gordon (1833–85), it was a bold and arguably rash decision to name a racehorse after him.

While Gordon was from a distinguished military family, the colt named after him was sold for an insulting 800 guineas as a yearling and showed himself to be worth no more. General Gordon ran just twice, finishing last both times.

As a human being, Gordon achieved far more but his name is always associated with his death, when Khartoum was captured by the Mahdi's forces two days before a relief force arrived.

This life is only one of a series of lives which our incarnation part has lived. I have little doubt of our having pre-existed.
General Gordon, 1877. He would, therefore, not have been surprised to learn that he was later reincarnated as a horse.

> **HENRY KISSINGER (1974)**
> • New Member • Charmer's Girl (Pappatea)

An enormous amount has been written about Henry Kissinger, quite a lot of it by Henry Kissinger, so it's surprising that so little has been said about how much taller his wife Nancy is than him. She's a lot taller. It may be of little significance, although it must make it impossible to share jumpers – and Henry Kissinger was a good one.

As a politician, Kissinger was a controversial figure but a highly influential one in shaping American foreign policy. Secretary of State from 1973 to 1977, during the final stages of the Vietnam War, in 1973 he was awarded the Nobel Peace Prize, although his critics thought that, instead, he should have been prosecuted for war crimes.

Mr Mansworth, Henry Kissinger's owner, was not among them. No doubt his opinion of Henry Kissinger became even more favourable over the years, peaking in 1981 when he won the Mackeson Gold Cup.

A very clever man, although not an endearing one, Kissinger possessed a disarming wit, which he used – to disarm. Still active at the age of 95, Kissinger is proof that a brain can remain bright for almost a century, perhaps longer.

No one will ever win the battle of the sexes; there's too much fraternising with the enemy.

Before the Freedom of Information Act, I used to say that, at meetings, 'The illegal we do immediately. The unconstitutional takes a little longer.'
At a meeting with Turkey's foreign minister, 1975

To be absolutely certain about something one must know everything or nothing about it.
Possibly spoken after the 2016 US Presidential Election

Races won: one hurdle race and 14 chases, notably the 1981 Mackeson Gold Cup, between 1978 and 1985.

JOHN WILKES – PART ONE (1970)
• Pall Mall • Ballerina (Preciptic)

As a racehorse, hopeless; as a man, extraordinary. You could write a book about him – several people have.

Famously ugly but charming and witty, John Wilkes (1725–97) led several lives in one. He boasted that it took him 'only half an hour to talk away my face'.

Wilkes made his name as a radical politician and journalist. High Sheriff of Buckingham, MP and eventually Lord Mayor of London, he was twice involved in duels, and expelled from Parliament for a seditious libel on King George III contained in the *North Briton*, a weekly magazine published by Wilkes. He championed a free press, electoral reform and American independence.

If you would care to turn to the Sexcetera chapter – oh, you already have – there is more.

> **Earl of Sandwich**: 'Sir, I do not know whether you will die on the gallows or of the pox.'
> **John Wilkes**: 'That depends, my lord, on whether I embrace your lordship's principles or your mistress.'

Races won: none. Hopeless as a two-year-old in 1972; ditto in 1973. He'd have been better off remaining human.

NON-WET (1980)
• Sallust • Maggie's Pet (Coronation Year)

As time passes, so does familiarity with once well-known political name tags. Hard to imagine, but there will come a time when mention of Brexiteers will be met with puzzlement. It may take a while.

Non-Wet was foaled the year after Margaret Thatcher became prime minister; a long and contentious premiership ensued. Thatcher's economic policy was soon in force. It involved tackling inflation, which was over 20 per cent, by cutting public expenditure, curbing pay rises – partly by taking on the hitherto powerful trade unions – raising interest rates and making a switch from direct taxes (notably income tax) to indirect ones (VAT was raised from eight per cent to 15 per cent).

The short-term result was a recession and rapid rise in unemployment. Unemployment remained high through the 1980s but inflation fell and economic growth was strong, at least in the service sector.

The policies were socially divisive and some members of Thatcher's first Cabinet were uneasy about their radical nature and speed of introduction. Ian Gilmour, Jim Prior and Peter Walker were prominent in this group and were known as 'Wets'. Those closer to Thatcher, including Chancellor of the Exchequer Geoffrey Howe and Chief Secretary to the Treasury John Biffen, were 'Dry'.

Non-Wet didn't have to worry about all that; as long as dinner arrived on time he was happy.

> Standing in the middle of the road is very dangerous: you get knocked down by the traffic from both sides.
> *Margaret Thatcher to Jim Prior during an argument which ended when Prior excused himself to attend the relaunch of Harold Macmillan's book,* The Middle Way. *The former Conservative prime minister would have been in the 'Wet' camp.*

Races won: twice, in 1983 and 1984.

SHAHRASTANI (1983)
* Nijinsky • Shademah (Thatch)

Most people think of Shahrastani (granted, most people have never heard of him, let alone thought about him), as the horse who won the 1986 Derby when he shouldn't have done, because Dancing Brave should have won it.

The Aga Khan was pleased because he owned Shahrastani. Long before Shahrastani became a horse he was a pioneering historian of religion. His great twelfth-century work – you may have read it – was *Kitab al-Milal wa al-Nihal* or The Book of Sects and Creeds.

Shahrastani (1086–1153) was notable for his objective approach to the study of religions. His magnum opus was translated into French as *Livre des Religions et des Sectes* and published in two volumes (1986 and 1993). If you can't read French, it may be a struggle.

Races won: four from seven in 1985 and 1986, notably the 1986 Derby and Irish Derby.

PETER THE GREAT (1972)
* Great Nephew * Ship Yard (Doutelle)

Rather cleverly named, as Peter the Great (1672–1725) was passionate about shipbuilding and created a powerful Russian navy.

One of the most impressive rulers of Russia, he was fortunate not to live to be 306, because he would have been appalled to learn that Timeform regarded him as 'of little account'.

The equine evidence for that verdict was strong but when Peter The Great was sent hurdling he did win the Wombat Challenge Cup at Newton Abbot in 1978. No other horse has been able to make the same claim.

ROBESPIERRE (2000)
* Polar Falcon * Go For Red (Thatching)

If only Maximilien Robespierre (1758–94) had heeded that expression, 'What goes around, comes around.' Having overseen the removal of thousands of heads during the French Revolution's most bloody period, the Reign of Terror, Robespierre's own head was removed in 1794. It was a relief for most people, although not, of course, for Robespierre.

The historian Thomas Carlyle famously referred to him as 'the sea-green incorruptible', so it was fitting that when Robespierre turned to racing his jockey wore the green colours of owners Dr and Mrs John Wilson.

Unfortunately, they didn't make Robespierre run fast enough to avoid defeat in all ten of his appearances in 2002 and 2003. Luckily, there was another Robespierre, in Germany.

> **ROBESPIERRE (2000)**
> • Dashing Blade • Royal Ascot (Pentathlon)

Better, winning four times in Germany between 2003 and 2005.

> Terror is nothing other than justice, prompt, severe, inflexible; it is therefore an emanation of virtue.
> *Robespierre, 'Sur les Principes de Morale Politique' (1794).*
> *Yeah, right.*

> **ROMMEL (1997)**
> • Baron Blakeney • Sizzling Sun (Sunyboy)

It is fitting that in racing, as in history, there have been several Rommels. The most widely accepted Rommel is that of the able and chivalrous Field Marshal Erwin Rommel (1891–1944), regarded as a 'good' German commander during the Second World War, a gentleman soldier whose involvement in the abortive 1944 plot to kill Hitler led to his suicide. (Rommel's, not Hitler's. That came later.)

Revisionist historians have painted a less flattering picture of Rommel but one that still compares favourably with his Nazi contemporaries and equine alter egos.

In Britain, Rommel was a flop. His score under Rules was

nought from five and, in point-to-points, one from 22. The one was at Kingston Blount in 2003.

It may be that he was best in North Africa, although in Australia, *Rommel (2011) Commands – I'mtoogoodtobetrue (Good And Tough)* fared better. His four wins embraced the Group 2 WA Guineas at Ascot in 2014 and Group 3 Zeditane Stakes at Caulfield the following year.

The best-named Rommel was *Rommels Gold (2002) Desert Fox – Suzy O'Neill (Gold Brose)*.

The Desert Fox was Rommel's nickname. I've no idea who Suzy O'Neill was but Rommels Gold won two small races at Murray Bridge and Mount Gambier in South Australia in 2009 and 2010, so I expect she was pleased.

> Certainly they are not good at war but one must not judge everyone in the world by his qualities as a soldier, otherwise we should have no civilisation.
> *Erwin Rommel to his son Manfred about Italians*

16. PLACES

In 1867 Queen Victoria laid the foundation stone for the Royal Albert Hall. She didn't really lay it but she wielded a trowel. Four years later the hall was opened and 98 years later Deep Purple played an unlikely concert there with the Royal Philharmonic Orchestra. Queen Victoria would not have been amused.

If you go, try to book seat 87 in row 11 of the K area of the stalls. It's right above the foundation stone and very near the spot where Queen Victoria held the trowel, although that went missing during the 1980s.

The Albert Hall has a rich history and one of its proudest moments came in 1958, when it appeared in an episode of *Hancock's Half Hour.*

> **Sid James**: 'I've been busy.'
> **Hilary St Clair** (Kenneth Williams): 'I know what you mean. It's been absolutely months since I've been to the Albert Hall.'
> **Sid James**: 'Yeah, me too.'
> **Tony Hancock**: 'He's talking about music, not all-in wrestling.'
> *'The Publicity Photograph' (1958)*

Races won: two in 1978, including the Thirsk Hunt Cup.

A tall story

Tall Story (1975)
• *Amazing* • *Spinning Yarn (Pantene)*
It took 26 runs before Tall Story was finally accepted into the winner's circle, at Aqueduct in 1979. He won there again the next year and at Belmont Park.

CANFORD CLIFFS (2007)
• Tagula • Mrs Marsh (Marju)

Named after an affluent bit of Dorset, next to Sandbanks, another affluent bit of Dorset where the redoubtable Louie Dingwall once trained horses on the sands.

Dingwall (1893–1982) never became affluent herself and her horses were generally of distinctly modest ability, unlike Canford Cliffs. He was owned by Robin Heffer, a wealthy meat merchant with an address in Canford Cliffs, and his children. Later, parts of Canford Cliffs were sold to others, including Coolmore. Perhaps Heffer's occupation encouraged Canford Cliffs to run faster.

He's the best I've ever had.
Trainer Richard Hannon senior after Canford Cliffs' victory in the 2011 Lockinge Stakes

Races won: 2009 Group 2 Coventry Stakes; 2010 Group 1 Irish 2,000 Guineas, St James's Palace Stakes, Sussex Stakes; 2011 Group 1 Lockinge Stakes and Queen Anne Stakes.

A rather hurtful name

Columnist (1977)
* *Swing Easy* • *Namecaller (Malicious)*
Won two races, in 1979 and 1981.

HATTA (1975)
* Realm • Sayorette (Sayajirao)

In 1967, while studying in Cambridge, Sheikh Mohammed bin Rashid Al Maktoum and his older brother Sheikh Hamdan went to Newmarket and saw Royal Palace win the 2,000 Guineas. The brothers were already enthusiastic horsemen but their father, Sheikh Rashid, the ruler of Dubai, kept them on a tight rein. They were in England to study, not to race horses.

It was almost ten years later, in 1976, that Sheikh Mohammed first ventured into Tattersalls' sales ring. He bought three yearlings, named them Hatta, Haddfan and Shaab, and sent them to trainer John Dunlop at Arundel in Sussex.

Hatta, named after a village in the Hajar Mountains, made her debut in a maiden race at Brighton on 20 June 1977. Sheikh Mohammed arrived by train and taxi to watch Ron Hutchinson give him his first winner in England. No one took much notice, even when Hatta went on to win the Group 3 Molecomb Stakes at Goodwood.

There was no sudden expansion of the Maktoums' string of thoroughbreds. It was 1979 before Shaab gave Sheikh Maktoum his first winner in England and 1980 before Sheikh Hamdan followed suit, with Mushref. In the same year, Sheikh Mohammed made his first purchases at Keeneland.

Hatta was the gentle breeze that grew into the hurricane that created the world's largest racing empire.

I have met this charming Arab, who would like to buy
a few horses. I think that, one day, he could be a very big
owner.
*Bloodstock agent Colonel Dick Warden, a friend and adviser
of Sheikh Mohammed*

Races won: 1977 Bevendean Maiden Stakes, Brighton, races at
Salisbury and Sandown, Group 3 Molecomb Stakes at Goodwood.

A clever name

Court Drinking (2007)
• *Alke* • *Royal Forum (Open Forum)*
Owned, appropriately, by the Illegal Racing Partnership, he suffered
from something, possibly a lack of ability, appearing only four times, to
no avail.

HEATH HOUSE (1977)
• Jimmy Reppin • Bell Heather (Langton Heath)

The Newmarket yard dates back to the seventeenth century.
Since 1970, Heath House has been the cherished base of one
of racing's most distinguished and characterful trainers, Sir
Mark Prescott.

A century earlier the stable's occupant was Mathew Dawson.
Dawson trained 28 Classic winners but arguably earned more fame
as the trainer of St Simon, who never ran in a Classic but in 1884
won both the Ascot Gold Cup and Goodwood Cup by 20 lengths,
and was never beaten. St Simon went on to be champion sire nine
times and sired 17 Classic winners.

St Simon is still at Heath House. At least his skin is, kept in
a glass frame by the walkway to the indoor school. The Natural
History Museum's archives for 1914 contain the record of an 'Offer
of skeleton of "St Simon" race horse owned by Duke of Portland'.

The offer was accepted, so part of St Simon is in Newmarket and part in London.

As a horse, Heath House was an insult to his own name. At least he had the decency to stay away from Heath House and, instead, make a nuisance of himself at Giles Beeson's yard in Sussex.

> Has ability but is very temperamental (unseated rider when swerving soon after start on first and final outings, wearing blinkers on latter); best left alone.
> *Timeform's* Racehorses of 1980. *Heath House was awarded Timeform's famous double squizzle – §§ – at that time denoting 'an arrant rogue or a thorough jade; so temperamentally unsatisfactory as to be not worth a rating'.*

Races won: what do you think?

Jolly good names that might as well go here as anywhere else

Giv Us A Smacker (1985)
* Smackover • Passionate (Woodborough)
Didn't have much of a chance, as only raced twice and missed both times.

Canoodle (2012)
* Stimulation • Flirtatious (Generous)
Congratulations to Mary Morrison, Canoodle's owner-breeder responsible, I imagine, for the filly's name. Trained by her husband Hughie Morrison, Canoodle has so far won a bumper race and two hurdle races.

HUMBER BRIDGE (1972)
* Decoy Boy * La Marseillaise (Alycidon)

It's a rum business, isn't it, naming a racehorse after a bridge? It may explain why Humber Bridge packed it in after one season, with the opening of the Humber Bridge still seven years away. Perhaps Mrs Jackson, who owned the horse, was a bridge enthusiast; perhaps Geoff Toft, who trained Humber Bridge at Beverley, not far north of the planned bridge, shared her enthusiasm.

Harold Wilson's Labour government didn't, until suddenly, during the campaign for the January 1966 Hull North by-election, Transport Secretary Barbara Castle announced that the long-delayed bridge would be built. The government had a wafer-thin majority and Hull North was a marginal seat. Labour held it.

The Humber Bridge was finally opened in 1981.

Will they ever bridge the Humber?
Will they ever span it or
Is it always an exception to the rule?
Is it such a privilege not to have a Humber Bridge
And to have to keep on going round by Goole?
*Chorus of 'The Humber Bridge Song' (1968) by Christopher
Rowe and Ian Clark*

Races won: two, in 1974.

Love it

Goldisocks (1978)
* *Le Coq d'Or* * *Red Stockings (Red Pins)*
He had his name to celebrate but no racecourse triumphs. Never mind: at least he had a nice name.

IKORODU ROAD (2003)
• Double Trigger • Cerisier (Roselier)

Given his name, Ikorodu Road was lucky to survive long enough to prove himself a capable chaser. Ikorodu Road is a notoriously dangerous expressway in Nigeria, more dangerous than the horse which, although occasionally parting with his rider, never ran into a car (I'm guessing).

Bought for 1,000 guineas as a foal, Ikorodu Road presumably spent his time eating and playing for the next five years before eventually being required to exert himself in a novice hurdle at Stratford. Starting at 100-1, Ikorodu Road was beaten a head.

He peaked in March 2012, winning over £29,000 for his owner, John Odell, in one handicap chase then, later in the month, winning over £31,000 in another chase. In all, Ikorodu Road, a stout stayer, won over £100,000. Not bad for a horse that cost £1,050.

The worst road in the world. There is an accident
every hour and death every day on that road.
An opinion expressed in Rosaline Odeh, Guns of Power
(2017)

Races won: five during a career lasting from 2008 to 2016.

A name, thrice

Rideitlikeustoleit (1999)
• *King's Signet* • *Fay Eden (Fayruz)*
After failing in point-to-points, in 2008 Rideitlikeustoleit failed in his sole attempt under Rules.

Rideitlikeustoleit (2005)
• *Dove Hunt* • *Sec Secrets (Triple Sec)*
Racing in New Mexico, Rideitlikeustoleit won at Sunland Park in 2007 and Ruidoso Downs in 2009.

Rideitlikeustoleit (2011)
* *Alamosa* • *Double Elle (Generous)*
On the other side of the world, in New Zealand, Rideitlikeustoleit has won five times so far.

KILMOGANY FIVE (1963)
* Aeolian • dam by Sandyman

A member of Cumbrian farmer and trainer John Dixon's staff told him that there was a horse worth seeing at Kilmoganny in County Kilkenny. When Dixon and his wife Ella went to Ireland they decided to look for themselves but there was a problem: the man who bred and owned the horse didn't have a phone. The only way to contact him was through the local shop. The number of McDonalds Grocery and Lounge Bar was Kilmoganny 5.

The Dixons returned to their base at Thursby with a horse they named after the shop's telephone number – minus an 'n'.

Kilmogany Five was a regular at northern racecourses during the late 1960s and early 1970s and won eight chases between 1969 and 1972. In recognition of his achievements, McDonalds produced a calendar featuring a photograph of the horse.

LAKE CONISTON (1991)
* Bluebird • Persian Polly (Persian Bold)

More often referred to as Coniston Water (see below), Lake Coniston, in the Lake District, sits below the Old Man of Coniston, so called because that's what you feel like when you reach the top.

Five miles long, the lake was a regular venue for Donald Campbell's obsessive attempts on the world water speed record, which he broke several times in *Bluebird* K7. On 4 January 1967 Campbell set off to push his own record of 276mph to 300mph. On an initial run he reached a speed of 311mph and averaged 297.6mph. On his return run, after reaching 320mph, *Bluebird*'s nose lifted, the boat flipped over backwards and Campbell was killed.

Ever since, his name and that of Lake Coniston have been inextricably linked. During 2000 and 2001 the wreckage and Campbell's body were recovered.

> The Old Man of Coniston retains a proud and dignified bearing, shedding his tears quietly into a lovely tarn at the base of the summit escarpment.
> *Alfred Wainwright,* A Pictorial Guide to the Lakeland Fells. The Southern Fells *(1960). Book Four in Wainwright's wonderful guide to walking in the Lake District.*

Races won: seven in 1994 and 1995, including the 1995 Group 1 July Cup and three Group 3 races.

CONISTON WATER (1989)
• Private Account • Rivers of Mist (Irish River)

Just the one win, in 1992, from a handful of races.

LAMBEAU FIELD (1994)
• Brass Minister • Romanero (Bravest Roman)

... and

LAMBEAU FIELD (2013)
• Cape Blanco • Xinji (Xaar)

An iconic location in American football: the home of the Green Bay Packers. Named after the team's founder and first coach, Lambeau Field is located in Green Bay, Wisconsin, near Lake Michigan.

Not only is it often very cold but Green Bay also has a population of only just over 100,000. It hasn't stopped the Packers from being one of the most successful teams in the NFL, with a unique ownership structure under which over 360,000 shareholders own the non-profit organisation. Also uniquely, fans have a habit of wearing cheesehead hats – yellow hats shaped like chunks of cheese, worn on the head. I think it might be Jarlsberg.

I had my first experience of American football at Lambeau Field in 1968. I didn't understand it and soon realised that when people said it was a bit like rugby they should have said, a tiny, weeny bit like it.

Having had one great quarterback in the shape of Brett Favre (1992–2007), Green Bay then had another – Aaron Rodgers (2008 to present).

> I tell my players every practice, 'Let's act like champions, let's practice like champions, let's play like champions, and let's be champions.'
> *Earl 'Curly' Lambeau, 1930*

Races won: it depends which Lambeau Field we're talking about. The 1994 one won 18 races between 1997 and 2003, mainly in Canada but latterly in California, Arizona and Texas.

The 2013 one hasn't won a thing yet and should be ashamed of himself.

17. THE BEST OF NAMES, THE WORST OF NAMES

THE 10 BEST

1. Wait For The Will (1996) *Seeking The Gold – You'd Be Surprised (Blushing Groom)*
2. One Over Parr (1972) *Reform – Seventh Bride (Royal Record)*
3. Step On Degas (1993) *Superpower – Vivid Impression (Cure The Blues)*
4. Au Renoir (2010) *Peintre Celebre – Goodbye (Efisio)*
5. That's Your Lot (1982) *Auction Ring – Guillotina (Busted)*
6. Geespot (1999) *Pursuit Of Love – My Discovery (Imperial Frontier)*
7. Court Drinking (2007) *Alke – Royal Forum (Open Forum)*
8. Sizzling Melody (1984) *Song – Mrs Bacon (Balliol)*
9. The Gatting Ball (2014) *Hard Spun – Art Of Deception (Artie Schiller)*
10. Regency Brighton (1978) *Royal Palace – Gay City (Forlorn River)*

First reserve

11. Coeur Blimey (2011) *Winged Love – Eastender (Opening Verse)*

THE 10 WORST

1. Gangrene (2002) *Bates Motel – Momento's Lady (Momento)*
2. Salmonella (1979) *Big Kohinoor – Kaysirmo (Dear Sir)*
3. Moron (1975) *Morston – One Extra (Abernant)*
4. Miss Rubbish (1978) *Rubor – Mishwish (Indian Ruler)*
5. Dishcloth (1974) *Fury Royal – Drishouge (Straight Deal)*
6. Bagapooh (2002) *Bag – Mertzie Pooh (Mertzon)*

7.   Semolina (1887) *St Simon – Mowerina (Scottish Chief)*
8.   Plastic Cup (1974) *Jukebox – Miss Melanie (Hard Ridden)*
9.   Steelworks (1978) *Steel Heart – Hariota (Hook Money)*
10. The Slug (2004) *Tamayaz – Snow Huntress (Shirley Heights)*

First reserve
11. Ebitda (2014) *Compton Place – Tipsy Girl (Haafhd)*

FIFTYSHADESOFHAY

FIFTYSHADESOFHAY (2010)
• Pulpit • Quiet Kim (Real Quiet)

A clever name thought up by the filly's three co-owners, Mike Pegram, Karl Watson and Paul Weitman and members of their families.

Inspired by EL James's bestselling erotic novel *Fifty Shades of Grey* (2011), Fiftyshadesofhay cost $175,000 as a yearling, whereas *Fifty Shades Of Grey* is available for £2.45 on Amazon. The filly also got whipped less than the novel's Anastasia Steele.

Trained by Bob Baffert, Fiftyshadesofhay was a good horse. She earned over $1 million in prize money and was sold for $1.3 million as a broodmare.

Races won: 2013 Grade 2 Black-Eyed Susan Stakes at Pimlico; 2014 Grade 2 Ruffian Stakes at Belmont plus two Grade 3 races.

FIFTY SHADES (2013)
• Tajraasi • Baylough Mist (Cloudings)

Despite lacking hay, has already won three jumps races in 2018.

FIFTYSHADESOFHAY IN FULL FLIGHT

ZEROESHADESOFGREY (2009)
* Portrait Gallery • Hazy Rose (Roselier)

Demonstrating that neither hay nor grey is essential for success, won seven jumps races between 2014 and 2016, and is still trying.

IT'S OVER

ITS OVER (1998)
• Grand Plaisir • Flemingtown Lady (Ovac)

Its Over won four jumps races in Ireland for owner-trainer Iggy Madden, all in 2004.

And now it really is over. Writing a book is like cooking a meal. It takes a long time to do but a short time to consume. Then someone says, 'I don't think much to this. Have you got anything else?'

No, although …

FURTHER READING

If you have enjoyed this book you may like to read other works by David Ashforth, including 'The Urban Poor Law' in D. Fraser (ed.), *The New Poor Law in the Nineteenth Century* (1976) and *Records of Achievement in the Market Place* (1990). There are others but most of them are about horseracing.

Or you could just watch another repeat of *Outnumbered*. The one with the German exchange student (series 4, episode 6, 2011) is the best. It's brilliant.

OUTNUMBERED (2013)
* Stowaway * Black Market Lass (Bob Back)

No good in 2017, ditto 2018.

INDEX

Popsi's Joy 75

Portland, 6th Duke of 43, 242

Posse 30

Potoooooo00 221–2

Potter, Beatrix 194–7

Potts, Alan and Ann 179–80

Powell, Stanley Kiran Gordon 73–4

Preakness Stakes 66, 162

Prescott, Sir Mark 202, 203, 242

Press Luncheon 115

Pretty Jewel 32–3

Priaprism 145

Priory Park 76

Prisoner of Zenda 104

Private Baldrick 85

Professor Plum 75, 76

Prufrock 106

Pull Your Socks Up 164

Punchestown racecourse 15, 69, 180

Pure Lust 145–6

Pussy 141–2

Qalibashi 70, 71

Quantitativeeasing 170–1

Queen Of The Tarts 152

Queenie 87

Queer Street 139–40

Quinlan Terry 202–3

Quisling 80

Racehorse 168

Radiotherapy 31–2

Rag Trade 35

Rainbird 141

Rainbow Quest 183

Randall, John 22–3, 159

Real Quiet 161–2

Record Token 113

Recuse 132

Red Alligator 208–9, 212

Red Candle 34

Red In Bed 230

Red Rum 35–6, 78, 179

Redcar racecourse 38, 95, 120, 170

Redlorryyellowlorry 170

Reed, Guy 66–7

Refused A Name 61

Regency Brighton 29, 249

Rekindling 187

Relkino 53, 68

Return 185

Reverend Green 75–6

Rhett Butler 138

Rhinestone Cowboy 188

Rhode Island Red 210

Rice-Davies, Mandy 89

Ricks Natural Star 54–5

Rideitlikeustoleit 245–6

Robespierre 236–7

Robin Hood 58

Roll-A-Joint 170

Rommel 237–8

Rommels Gold 238

Rose To Fame 133

Ross-Hume, Mabel 13

Rowe, Richard 57

Royal Axminster 172

Royal Dartmouth 172

Royal Devon 172

Royal Palace 241